AIRBUS
A380

2005 to present

Dedication

To my daughter Hannah – may this remarkable aircraft, and others like it, take you to new places and adventures the world over.

First published in November 2017

Robert Wicks has asserted his moral right to be identified as the author of this work.

A catalogue record for this book is available from the British Library.

ISBN 978 1 78521 108 9

Library of Congress control no. 2017933528

Published by Haynes Publishing,
Sparkford, Yeovil, Somerset BA22 7JJ, UK.
Tel: 01963 440635
Int. tel: +44 1963 440635
Website: www.haynes.com

Haynes North America Inc.
859 Lawrence Drive, Newbury Park, California 91320, USA.

While every effort is taken to ensure the accuracy of the information given in this book, no liability can be accepted by the author or publishers for any loss, damage or injury caused by errors in, or omissions from, the information given.

Printed in Malaysia

COVER CUTAWAY ILLUSTRATION:
A380 Airbus. *(Alex Pang)*

AIRBUS A380

2005 to present

Owners' Workshop Manual

Insights into the design, construction, operation and maintenance of the world's most recognised and talked about airliner

Robert Wicks

Contents

Author's note and acknowledgements

Author's note

The first time I ever flew in an aircraft was in South Africa in 1985. It was a bumpy 90-minute flight in a rather rickety old Douglas DC-3 from a small airfield near Pietersburg to Johannesburg.

By then, my love affair with flying was all-encompassing and rather varied: I can recall riding my motorcycle to that same airfield to watch light aircraft on their final approach; I created detailed technical sketches of aircraft on a drawing board I still have today; I had a giant poster of the Concorde's remarkable cockpit pinned up on my bedroom wall; and I recall being given the opportunity to sit in a South African Air Force Dassault Mirage F1 and an Impala MKII. A trip to the UK in the early 1990s was planned to coincide with the Farnborough Air Show – whenever there was a chance to see or somehow be involved with aircraft, I was there. Farnborough remains a regular date on my calendar as does the Royal International Air Tattoo. Being at an airport is never a chore – always a treat.

My own plans to fly fast jets never quite came off, but I have been fortunate to channel my passion in other ways, predominantly through photography and the writing of books. Three years ago I was granted unprecedented levels of access to Heathrow Airport and was fortunate to write a book on day-to-day operations at one of the world's busiest airports.

When the opportunity arose with Haynes to follow this up with a book on the Airbus A380, I leapt at the chance. I had followed the launch back in 2007 with great anticipation and have been fortunate enough to fly on the aircraft many times. Even if you're sitting in the economy cabin, it's a unique experience and regular flyers will notice the discernible difference when aboard this double-decker, wide-body, four-engine airliner that still turns heads at airports the world over.

As I came to learn, the A380 is packed from nose to tail and wingtip to wingtip with some of aviation's great innovations, pushing the boundaries of what the industry thought possible. It is much of this technology, as well as the ground-breaking production operation, which intrigued me the most when writing about the aircraft.

It's fair to say the A380, or rather the Airbus strategy of building an aircraft of such scale, has come in for criticism. To make matters worse, the current slump in orders is not helping, but by the time you have read from cover to cover, I expect you will agree that the changes we are seeing in the global aviation market mean the aircraft has a very bright future indeed and is simply ahead of its time.

Writing this book has been a real privilege and one of the most remarkable experiences in my life. Whether you are simply an enthusiast, a past or future passenger, or from within the industry itself, I hope the book informs, enlightens and entertains – welcome aboard!

BELOW Author Robert Wicks prepares for take-off in the British Airways A380 simulator at Heathrow.

Acknowledgements

First and foremost, my thanks must go to Robert Gage, the Head of Media Relations at Airbus in the UK, who has championed and supported the development of this book and assisted in navigating some of the complexities of the wider Airbus organisation. Robert's introduction to John Roberts, the former Chief Engineer on the A380 for wing, fuel and landing gear systems, proved extremely valuable – not only has John been a great font of knowledge for my wide range of queries, but he has also kindly written the foreword.

Undoubtedly one of the most fascinating parts of writing this book was the opportunity for an up close and personal visit to see the *convoi exceptionnel* which transports the various major components of the A380 to the Final Assembly Line (FAL) in Toulouse. My thanks go to Victoria Runcie and Phil McGraa at Airbus in the UK for facilitating this once-in-a-lifetime experience. It's only when one sees the aircraft in this form, traversing narrow roads through the countryside in the black of night that the A380's scale can truly be appreciated.

On site at the FAL, I was treated to a full tour and fortunate to be accompanied by Richard Carcaillet who, for 10 years (2003–13) was in charge of A380 marketing.

Back in the UK, Richard Goodfellow from British Airways (BA), kindly provided the opportunity to witness a complete A380 turnround. This was an enormously valuable visit – detailed in some length in Chapter 8 – with access to the aircraft, the maintenance team, flight crew and the Turnround Manager to see first-hand how, in just 3 hours, an inbound A380 can be prepared for its outbound journey.

On the flight deck during the turnround was Khalid Murad from BA Engineering and despite his busy schedule he was able to offer great insight into various technical aspects of this remarkable aircraft.

My thanks go to both Simon Newbold and Rachel Betts at Heathrow Airport for facilitating the visit. The pair were great supporters of my earlier Haynes Manual on the airport itself and were only too happy to help again on this occasion.

ABOVE The A380 is a regular sight at airports around the world and continues to turn heads. *(Engine Alliance)*

Tony Cane from the BA Communications Department helped on various fronts, including a visit to the airline's maintenance base where I was able to spend time with and learn some valuable details from Aircraft Maintenance Supervisor, Derek Cogswell.

Tony also kindly arranged a visit to BA's Global Learning Academy based at Heathrow where I met Geof Fearon and Andy Clubb who together provided some great insight on the flight deck as well as the rather unexpected opportunity to fly the BA A380 simulator – the closest I'll ever get to the real thing and apologies again for that hard landing!

On an Airbus media trip I met photographer Martyn Cartledge, and some of his images appear in the book, as do a few from the talented Waldo van der Waal.

The book would not have been possible without the support of the editorial team at Haynes and I am indebted to Senior Commissioning Editor Jonathan Falconer who has been very supportive throughout the past 12 months.

On a final note, my sincere thanks go to the very talented team of graphic artists Roy Scorer, Alex Pang and Rolando Ugolini, whom together have been able to bring the A380 to life through their imaginative and insightful drawings.

I hope you enjoy the read.

Robert Wicks
July 2017

Foreword

by John Roberts

The huge increase in travelling by air over the last 50 years has changed the world in many ways. Most of us have been lucky enough to visit places and people in faraway countries that would only have been possible for the lucky few in previous generations. In 2015 over 3 billion passengers were flown by the world's airlines.

How many of that huge number have sat in airport terminals, looked at those aircraft outside and marvelled at the engineering and scientific endeavour that gives them the ability to move us quickly and safely over vast distances?

Over the last half-century, though, most of those travellers would have been unable to identify the type of aeroplane that would transport them and I would suggest that there have perhaps only been three passenger aircraft that are universally recognised.

Two of those first flew in 1969 and were part of the great step in engineering confidence that occurred in that decade. They are the BAC/Sud Aviation Concorde and the Boeing 747 jumbo. These two aircraft have had a very different effect on the lives of travellers but are instantly recognisable to all.

The Boeing 747 had a dramatic effect on long-range mass transportation, allowing long-distance travel to be achieved at a reasonable cost. Nearly 50 years later a much-updated but visually similar aeroplane is still in production. Concorde of course never had the commercial success of the Boeing 747 but will always be remembered as an icon of that era. Both of these aircraft are worthy of books of their own and the volumes in the same series as this are recommended.

Concorde left an oft-forgotten legacy to the world of aviation; it gave lessons to the European industry on how to work together to produce an aeroplane. In turn, those lessons have fed into what has become Airbus, a company of equal size and strength to its American competitor, Boeing.

Some 36 years after the first flight of Concorde and the jumbo jet, the next aircraft to capture our collective imagination took to the skies. That aircraft is the Airbus A380, yet only a small part of what it took to deliver it is visible.

Robert Wicks has written this book based on many hours of interviews, research and investigation to give an insight into this iconic aircraft. This fascinating story is that of the many skilled people who designed her, manufactured her, tested her and who operate and maintain her.

As with all major steps forward in engineering,

RIGHT Former A380 Chief Engineer at Airbus in the UK, John Roberts, specialised in developing the aircraft's wing, fuel and landing gear systems.

the achievement has not always been easy. This book explains that achievement so that next time you look out of the window at the airport terminal a much greater appreciation can be had on the work of the people who put it there and operate it on a daily basis.

The Airbus A380 is one of very few engineering designs that is recognisable wherever it is seen. Robert has given us the opportunity to more fully understand her story.

John Roberts graduated from Brunel University, London, in 1978 with a degree in Mechanical Engineering and joined Dowty Fuel Systems working on control equipment for jet engines. In 1992 he joined British Aerospace Airbus in Bristol as Chief Systems Engineer. Five years later he became the UK Chief Engineer for the A330/340 programme. After a period at Messier-Dowty as Vice President of Engineering, he rejoined Airbus as the UK Chief Engineer for the A380, a position he held through the challenging period of the aircraft's early in-service life. Since retiring, John has acted as a consultant to companies in Europe and North America. He lives in Gloucestershire and is married with three children.

ABOVE Qantas is one of 13 international airlines operating the A380 today. *(Airbus)*

BELOW MSN 004 puts on a flying display for the crowds at the 2016 Farnborough International Air Show. *(Author)*

Chapter 1

The super jumbo

OPPOSITE This Etihad A380 aptly demonstrates the aircraft's imposing size. *(Airbus)*

Introduction

The Airbus A380 is not only the world's largest passenger aircraft, it is also an extraordinary tale of engineering imagination. Everything about it is gigantic – from its incredible passenger numbers to its vast wingspan, from the size of its global supply chain to the expansive manufacturing facilities and logistics operation. This is an aircraft like no other.

Given its scale, Airbus had little choice but to go back to the drawing board to design the A380 completely from scratch, with many commentators holding the view that it should be regarded – in aviation terms – as major a technological achievement as Concorde was back in the mid-1960s. Few believed it was possible – including some of the engineers based at the Airbus facility in Toulouse who brainstormed the original project in the summer of 1988. It was a fascinating time in the aviation sector – the Cold War was coming to an end and a new political era of increased global freedom was emerging, which heralded growing potential for international travel and trade. The so-called 'Tiger' economies of Asia-Pacific were expanding rapidly, business in Europe was strong and air passenger traffic was showing steady, year-on-year growth.

Increasing passenger demands meant more aircraft in already crowded airspace and even more pressure on many already congested airports, particularly in key locations such as Hong Kong and Japan.

Airbus and its US rival, Boeing, initially had similar ideas on how to deal with the challenges that lay ahead but, over time, their philosophies grew further and further apart. Airbus eventually took the plunge in what many describe as one of the riskiest bets in the aerospace industry, owing to the complexity of its development and its elaborate manufacturing process.

What Airbus finally produced is nothing short of remarkable, with major innovations in aerodynamics, structures, systems, integration and manufacturing, all of which have contributed to the success of the aircraft.

Today the A380 has the lowest cost-per-seat of any large aircraft and one of the super jumbos takes off or lands every 2 minutes – quite an achievement since the launch of the aircraft ten years ago in 2007 with Singapore Airlines.

Serious questions have been asked of the project – which is estimated to have cost Airbus around £17bn in development costs – and it is well documented that demand for the aircraft has fallen some way below the manufacturer's expectations. This has slowed production on

the FAL in Toulouse and left many wondering about the future of the A380. Talk to Airbus executives, though, and their commitment to the aircraft is unwavering – their belief in what started all those years ago remains firm.

Over the next two decades, several new large-scale airports will develop to serve new cities that are emerging on the back of rapid urbanisation, especially in Asia, while congestion at more established airports like Heathrow will reach breaking point. It is here that the aircraft will make its most valuable contribution as its capability is critical to ensuring that the relentless increase in long-haul flights between the world's busiest airports is handled as effectively and efficiently as possible.

ABOVE Singapore Airlines was the first airline customer for the A380 in 2007. *(Airbus)*

LEFT Malaysia Airlines was the eighth carrier to operate the A380 with an inaugural flight from Heathrow to Kuala Lumpur. *(Airbus)*

ABOVE Airbus is an international pioneer in the aerospace industry. *(Airbus)*

BELOW The company operates across the aerospace sector with interests in commercial aircraft, helicopters, defence and space. *(Airbus)*

About Airbus

The A380 is produced by the civil aircraft manufacturing division of Airbus. Based in Blagnac, France, on the outskirts of Toulouse, Airbus has production and manufacturing facilities in France, Germany, Spain, China, the United Kingdom and the United States. The company employs more than 72,000 staff across the wider organisation, which includes a division focused on defence and space and another on helicopters.

Airbus began as a consortium of aerospace manufacturers, Airbus Industrie in 1970 between France's Aerospatiale and Deutsche Airbus, while Spain's CASA joined shortly after, followed by British Aerospace in 1979. The co-operation was initiated with considerable government involvement to take on successful US manufacturers Boeing, Douglas and Lockheed who were enjoying a dominant position with Europe's aviation sector still flagging after the Second World War.

The companies operated fairly independently until Airbus became a single, fully integrated company in 2001, 80% owned by the European Aeronautic Defence and Space Company (EADS), a merger of the French, German and Spanish interests, and 20% by BAe Systems, the successor to British Aerospace.

In January 2014, EADS was reorganised as Airbus Group, combining the divisions for development and marketing of civil and military aircraft, as well as communications systems, missiles, space rockets, helicopters, satellites and related systems.

The company produces and markets several highly successful families of aircraft: the single-aisle A320 family; the wide-body, long-range A330; the all-new next-generation A350 XWB and – of course – the double-decker A380. In 2004 Airbus outstripped Boeing for the first

time in terms of number of aircraft delivered and orders taken.

The company's 10,000th aircraft, an A350, was delivered to Singapore Airlines in October 2016. At the same time it was estimated the global Airbus fleet had performed more than 110 million flights over some 215 billon km, carrying some 12 billion passengers.

Airbus has built on its strong European heritage to become truly international – with roughly 180 locations and 12,000 direct suppliers globally. The company has aircraft and helicopter final assembly lines across Asia, Europe and the Americas, and has achieved a more than sixfold order book increase since 2000.

Airbus in numbers:

- 688 – aircraft delivered by Airbus in 2016
- 6,874 – number of aircraft on the Airbus order book
- 10 – years it will take Airbus to fulfil the order book at current production rates.

A380 origins

The design of any new airliner is a significant undertaking and begins years before its first flight as the development lifecycle graphic demonstrates. Perhaps appropriately for a super jumbo, the A380's gestation period was a long one, with Airbus engineers based in Toulouse looking at the possibility of building an aircraft capable of carrying 600–800 passengers as far back as 1988.

The development team, led by Jean Roeder, began work in secret in the late 1980s on the development of an ultra-high-capacity airliner (UHCA). The motivation for the project was twofold. Firstly, the UHCA would complete the Airbus range of products, enabling it to become a global player in the aviation market. Secondly, it would break the dominance that Boeing had enjoyed in this market segment since the early 1970s with its iconic and much-loved 747 jumbo jet.

Plans were formally announced at the 1990 Farnborough Air Show, with the stated goal of building a high-capacity aircraft capable of delivering 15% lower operating costs than Boeing's stalwart.

It's worth noting that the financial strain of

developing the 747 almost brought Boeing to its knees, but the massive leap in capacity it offered compared with the next biggest plane available (the McDonnell Douglas DC-8), transformed both the experience and the economics of long-haul flying. More than 1,500 have been built and Boeing's gamble eventually reaped rich rewards.

Despite the existing plans, two of the partners in the initial Airbus consortium – Daimler-Benz and British Aerospace – pushed for co-operation with Boeing on what prosaically came to be known as a new Very Large Commercial Transport (VLCT) aircraft. It was apparent that neither company wanted to compete head-on over a project of this scale, given the inherent risks.

By January 1993, the two rivals started a joint feasibility study for the VLCT aircraft with a view to forming a partnership to share the limited market. The study concluded that compared to the 747, the new aircraft should have significantly more capacity, increased range and passenger comfort. It also had to be considerably more efficient (up to 20% lower operating costs) and, in a more environmentally conscious society, it had to burn less fuel and be a lot quieter than the forerunner.

Reaching consensus on building the VLCT was a tricky affair and Boeing seemed intent on producing a plane substantially bigger than the 747, which would complement rather than replace it. Airbus executives became impatient and realised that as long as there was no agreement on how to build the VLCT, Boeing could continue to milk its 747 monopoly.

ABOVE Today, an A380 takes off or lands every two minutes. (*Airbus*)

ABOVE During the development phase, consensus converged on a double-deck layout that provided more passenger volume than a traditional single-deck design. *(Airbus)*

With hopes of a joint venture fading fast, Airbus eventually plucked up the courage to go it alone and in 1995 the two rivals went their separate ways. Boeing announced plans for its successor to the 747 – the 747X – a stretched version with the signature 'hump' extended rearwards to accommodate more passengers. Various factors, including the cost to design and engineer a new wing, brought Boeing's plans to a halt within two years.

Airbus formed a self-contained Large Aircraft Division to progress its plans for developing a very large airliner – designated the A3XX – and soon realised that an aircraft of the size envisioned would need the biggest wings ever constructed.

The manufacturer commenced meetings with prospective airline customers and the feedback convinced executives there was indeed a large market for a modern plane capable of carrying between 550 and 650 passengers up to 9,000 miles (15,000km). With market forecasts indicating that air travel was likely to grow by about 5% a year, the demand for high-capacity aircraft could reach around 1,235 by 2020, reaffirming the view that there was a clear market for a super jumbo.

At the 1996 Farnborough Air Show, Airbus unveiled plans for the A3XX designed to challenge Boeing's monopoly, claiming it to be the only solution to growing airport congestion.

RIGHT From the drawing board to the skies – when Airbus announced the aircraft would be launched, it secured 50 firm orders from six customers. *(Airbus)*

Development costs at the time were quoted at £5.4bn.

Several design options were considered, including an odd side-by-side combination of two fuselages from the A340 but consensus eventually converged on a double-decker layout that provided more passenger volume than a traditional single-deck design. With the concept defined and agreed, the supervisory board of newly restructured Airbus voted to launch a £7.6bn programme to build the A3XX, rechristened as the A380, with 50 firm orders from 6 launch customers.

The A380 designation was a break from previous Airbus families, which had progressed sequentially from A300 to A340. It was chosen because the number 8 resembles the double-deck cross-section, and is a lucky number in some Asian countries where the aircraft was being marketed.

A key player in the aircraft's development was Robert Lafontan, whose career began at Avions Marcel Dassault/Breguet Aviation in 1977. In 1989 he joined Aérospatiale, working on the A319/A320/A321 programmes and was subsequently appointed Vice-President of Engineering at the Airbus Large Aircraft Division (A3XX) and A3XX Chief Engineer in 1996. When the A380 launched in 2000 Robert was appointed A380 Programme Chief Engineer and had the rather unique experience of being responsible for the aircraft's development from its project phase right through to certification and entry into service.

Seven weeks before its official launch, the fast-growing Dubai-based airline Emirates showed its faith in the project by declaring that it would buy ten A380s. Little did Airbus know back then just how important this relationship would be for the future of the aircraft.

The aircraft configuration was finalised in early 2001, and manufacturing of the first A380 wing box component started in January 2002. The milestone was celebrated against a backdrop of spiralling development costs which reached £9.5bn by the time the first aircraft was completed.

The first A380, serial number MSN001 and registration F-WWOW, was unveiled in Toulouse on 18 January 2005. It took its maiden flight three months later on 27 April 2005, flying from Toulouse Blagnac International Airport with a

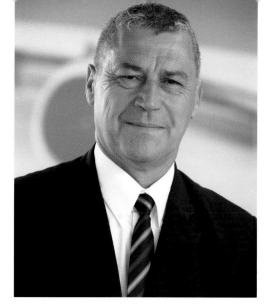

crew of six headed by Chief Test Pilot Jacques Rosay. On landing, Rosay said flying the A380 had been 'like handling a bicycle'.

The A380 had been born.

The aircraft development lifecycle

To develop a new aircraft takes a huge investment in terms of people and money over many years. This investment will be measured in billions of dollars. To manage the risk in that investment the manufacturer follows a comprehensive process known as the development lifecycle. This process covers everything from initial concept design to materials testing, wind tunnel testing, engine specification and procurement, landing gear and wing tests, fuel testing and, ultimately, flight testing. Looking at the Airbus approach to this, their view is that the lifecycle's guiding principle is to provide 'key deliverables' at each milestone. These are called maturity gates (MGs), and they range from MG1 to MG15.

The process is intended to ensure all the various requirements for a new aircraft are understood, defined and achieved. It must meet all the safety requirements, and be able to make money for the operator and the manufacturer.

Once the market demand for an aircraft of the size of the A380 was established, the process was started. Initially the plane was referred to as the A3XX.

The Feasibility Phase (MG1 to MG3) is when the programme's overall objectives and assumptions are defined and the basic architecture and decision solution rankings are

In recent years there have been contrasting views from Airbus and Boeing, as well as many airlines they supply, when it comes to how passengers prefer to travel and the aircraft needed to satisfy this demand. The A380 is very much at the centre of this debate.

The differences of opinion essentially boil down to frequency versus capacity and in aviation terms, this is often referred to as the hub-and-spoke philosophy versus the point-to-point approach.

Hub-and-spoke sees passengers flying in larger aircraft to big hub airports and then taking short-haul flights to their final destinations. The alternative point-to-point option necessitates more direct flights between destinations and it means airlines have a difficult choice, with manufacturers offering aircraft both with greater range and more capacity.

Historically, Airbus's rival Boeing has taken the view that today's passengers prefer more point-to-point flights, flown more frequently on smaller aircraft. They point to the drying-up of orders for passenger versions of the 747 as evidence for this and have put the likes of the new generation of twin engine 787 Dreamliners

BELOW Emirates have created a long-haul transfer hub in Dubai, capable of connecting most parts of the globe using long-haul aircraft, for which the A380 is ideally suited.
(Airbus)

and their venerable 777 workhorses at the centre of their strategy.

Through the A380, Airbus leads the way in the very large capacity segment and takes a different view, arguing that the approach of their American rivals means burning more fuel per passenger, putting more strain on overloaded air-traffic control systems and creating more congestion at airports that are already finding it difficult to cope.

The A380 certainly complements the hub-and-spoke system based on the assumption that airlines will continue to fly smaller planes on shorter routes (spokes) into a few large hubs, then onward to the next hub. They see this as a key strategy, especially between large city pairs between Asia, Europe and North America.

That said, the lines are blurring and it's fair to say Airbus is positioning the A380 as much as a point-to-point, as a hub-and-spoke aircraft with the manufacturer's marketing teams trying to sell the aircraft on multiple routes. Ultimately, it's a debate that will run for some time as one doesn't exclude the other and it will be a case of 'horses for courses'.

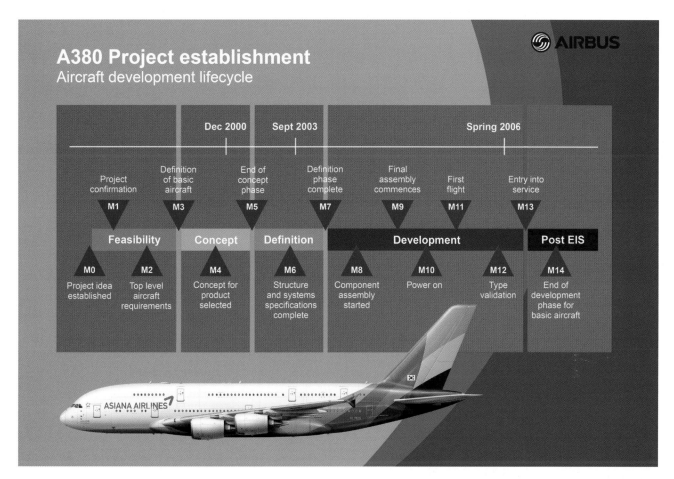

A380 Project establishment
Aircraft development lifecycle

	Dec 2000	Sept 2003		Spring 2006

Project confirmation	Definition of basic aircraft	End of concept phase	Definition phase complete	Final assembly commences	First flight	Entry into service
M1	M3	M5	M7	M9	M11	M13

Feasibility		Concept	Definition	Development			Post EIS

M0	M2	M4	M6	M8	M10	M12	M14
Project idea established	Top level aircraft requirements	Concept for product selected	Structure and systems specifications complete	Component assembly started	Power on	Type validation	End of development phase for basic aircraft

made in response to customer needs. Potential new technologies are chosen, industrial scenarios are examined and the initial team that will drive development in the Concept Phase is established.

At this stage potential customers for the plane are asked to join in discussions to agree what the requirements are for the plane. The Concept Phase (MG3 to MG5) includes several major decisions, such as validation of aircraft performance targets, selection of the structure and systems architecture, authorisation of resource ramp-ups and confirmation of the industrial launch. Key deliverables are defined, including the aircraft design, build and component concepts, plus performance and commercial margins.

At the end of 2000 the development programme had reached a point where contracts with customers could be made. This is the Authorisation to Offer approval taken at the highest level within Airbus. After contracts are signed the performance requirements for the plane are frozen.

During this phase, the suppliers – many of whom work with Airbus through the entirety of the development lifecycle – are selected. Initially, several potential suppliers competing on the same work packages are co-located with Airbus teams, all of them working in a fully integrated way, using the same systems, tools and design processes. Suppliers are then chosen for specific work packages during the Joint Definition Phase.

Discussions take place with airworthiness regulators (EASA and FAA) on how Airbus will meet the necessary safety requirements.

The A380 development process took longer than normal as there were a large number of potential design iterations. Further challenges came from the need to meet specific requirements to enable operations at airports with minimal changes to existing infrastructure.

In addition, the size of the plane meant that a lot of work was needed to make sure it could be manufactured and transported to Toulouse. It had to fit on barges, boats and trucks and through small French villages.

ABOVE Any new aircraft – particularly one as complex and innovative as the A380 – requires careful planning and development, with key deliverables reached at each milestone. *(Author)*

RIGHT The upper deck on MSN 004 – the flight-test aircraft has no cabin furnishing. *(Author)*

BELOW A view of the main deck on MSN 004 – all the systems cables and ducting mounted between the floors are visible to allow inspection and easy attachment of flight-test instruments. *(Author)*

The aircraft truly takes shape in the Design Phase (MG5 to MG7), when the overall design and cabin definitions are frozen, the first parts have been made and all critical design reviews have been passed.

This phase also features the bulk of the Industrial and Test Means Development Phases. With the launch of the Industrial Development Phase, the first elements are designed, produced and qualified for the initial aircraft assembly. The manufacturing system – including manufacturing and assembly plants, final assembly line, jigs and tools, testing, transportation and plant logistics – are prepared and assessed to ensure that the programme will meet its industrial schedule. Furthermore, the testing means – virtual testing and simulators, laboratory benches, static and fatigue test specimens and flight test instrumentation – are designed and produced.

So significant was the scale of the A380 project – including the complex production and logistics arrangements – that it resulted in a series of organisational and procedural changes at Airbus.

During the final phases (MG7 to MG15), the aircraft is built, and intensive tests – including flight trials – are performed in parallel. The objective is to assemble, certify and deliver a fully mature aircraft, starting with the programme's launch customer. At this point series production can begin.

To ensure a smooth entry into service, the first operators' pilots, cabin crew and

ABOVE An example of the many kilometres of instrumentation wiring added for flight-tests. *(Author)*

ABOVE RIGHT The flight-test engineers' station – from here they can see all the data coming from the aircraft as well as the actions of the flight crew. The test data is transmitted to Airbus teams on the ground in real time. *(Author)*

RIGHT Flight-test planes such as this A380 often use water ballast tanks (visible in the background) to imitate the weight of passengers and their baggage. The water can be pumped around the system to provide a variety of centre of gravity positions. *(Airbus)*

LEFT The A380 underwent cold weather trials in Iqualit, Canada, to prove all its systems work in freezing conditions. *(Airbus)*

There were five aircraft used in the Airbus flight-test programme: 001, 004, 002, 009 and 007.

■ MSN 001 was the first to fly on 27 April 2005; early flights went so well the aircraft was actually displayed at the Paris Air Show a mere six weeks later, and MSN 004 was the second. Both were loaded with so-called heavy flight-test instrumentation and were used extensively for early development work e.g. flight envelope opening, performance and environmental tests (cold weather, hot and high and extreme operational tests). MSN 001 was fitted with Rolls-Royce engines and subsequently went on to be used as the test aircraft for the Rolls-Royce Trent XWB-84 and XWB-97 engines. It was, in fact, mandatory for certification purposes to have the two engines on offer flight-tested, but that was ultimately done with MSN 009. MSN 004 was re-engined to Engine Alliance (EA) from Rolls-Royce after its flight-test mission for certification was completed, to have both engines on a test A380 in case of an operational or engine-related flight-testing requirement that might have arisen after Entry Into Service (EIS).

■ MSN 002 was a pre-production aircraft with a variety of modifications, but not quite full production standard. It was the cabin test aircraft (with 'medium FTI') to test all cabin systems. It performed the 'early long flights', real-life, up to 12hr-long flights with passengers (Airbus employees) on board intensively testing all cabin systems. At one stage there was interest in the aircraft from a private customer but the order was cancelled. It is currently being stored in Toulouse and is expected to go on display at the Aeroscopia Museum adjacent to the airport.

■ MSN 007 was another full-cabin A380 (Rolls-Royce powered), which was extensively used in very successful customer demo flights/demo tours throughout 2007 when it visited customers, potential customers, and other events like air shows.

■ Following the wing rib feet micro-cracking issue on some, not all, wing ribs, MSN 004 had one wing modified with the upgrade while the other was left unmodified. Strain gauges on each wing provided detailed comparisons of the solution to validate the definitive solution prior to implementation 'under warranty' on the in-service fleet (now completed). MSN 004 has been a regular visitor to international air shows, including Paris and Farnborough, and has now been pledged to the Le Bourget Musée de l'Air et de l'Espace.

■ MSN 003 and MSN 005 were mainly used for proving cabin system functionality. They were later refurbished and went into service. Both are with Singapore Airlines, the former being the first A380 to enter service and the latter being delivered in January 2008. These were the first two production-standard A380s. Later on, MSN 007 and 009 were refurbished, re-engined with EA engines, and re-delivered to Emirates who had purchased them.

This table summarises the A380 flight-test fleet:

BELOW MSN 004 over Farnborough in 2016 – one of five development aircraft produced by Airbus. *(Author)*

Aircraft	Flight no	Flight hours	Take-off
A380 MSN 001	417	1,316:00	1,139
A380 MSN 004	383	1,048:45	913
A380 MSN 002	92	506:50	121
A380 MSN 007	40	180:40	46
A380 MSN 009	111	370:25	196
Total	1,043	3,422:40	2,415

maintenance staff train within Airbus facilities, and all the customer support means, spares, tools and documentation are deployed in time for the first airline operations.

As the A380 was so large the prototype aircraft visited airports around the world to confirm that there would be no issues in operation.

After all the paperwork and testing is complete, the airworthiness authorities issue the aeroplane with a certificate to say it can be used to carry passengers. With that, deliveries to the airlines can start.

Once the processes for industrial production are streamlined and running robustly and operational feedback has been received, the development project is closed and the programme is transformed into the series production mode. The lessons learned are taken and shared with following development projects and the lifecycle begins again.

ABOVE A certified A380 departs for its entry into service with Emirates in Dubai. *(Airbus)*

BELOW An A380 earmarked for Etihad Airways rolls out from the paint shop in Hamburg. *(Airbus)*

ABOVE The Royal Air Force aerobatic team – the famous Red Arrows – puts on a fly past with the A380. (Airbus)

A380 TIMELINE

1970 Airbus is founded.

1991 With a working designation of A3XX, initial exploratory discussions take place about the potential for and requirements of a super jumbo.

1993 Boeing confirms it is interested in collaborating on a Very Large Aircraft (VLA) programme with Airbus, but just six months later the US manufacturer elects to favour smaller aircraft and the Airbus partners are left to go it alone.

1996 The 'Airbus Large Aircraft Division' is founded.

2000 Commercial launch of the A3XX.

2001 The Airbus consortium is restructured as an integrated entity.

2002 Component manufacture begins.

2004 Rolls-Royce delivers the first engine, airports commence with structural changes to deal with the A380's impending arrival, final assembly commences in Toulouse and Airbus announces that the project's development costs are likely to be considerably more expensive than anticipated.

2005 A long-running dispute between Airbus and Boeing over unfair competition and state subsidies is settled in January and three months later the A380 has its maiden flight from Toulouse with a 12-month test programme to follow. By mid-year, Airbus is forced to announce a six-month delay to production.

2006 In June Airbus faces a similarly long production delay and then a further delay of a year is announced in October.

2007 Launch customer Singapore Airlines takes delivery of its first aircraft and the A380 officially enters service.

Market trends

Much of Airbus's belief in the A380 representing the solution for dealing with some of aviation's most pressing issues is based on the expected doubling of air passenger traffic over the next 15 years.

The aircraft manufacturer predicts that VLA will reach some 3,400 flights a day out of 200 airports around the world. About 70% of those flights, however, will emanate from just 25 airports, many in Asia.

Interestingly, today 54% of A380 capacity in the way of weekly seats offered is from, to or within Asia and between now and 2035, Airbus predicts that 50% of the top traffic flows will involve Asia-Pacific, with the flow of domestic flights within China at the top of the rankings. Domestic traffic in India is also expected to grow more than fivefold over the next 20 years. With this in mind, Airbus forecasts that by 2023 there will be 1,262 VLA in operation.

The growth in the number of airports capable of servicing the A380 has increased steadily over the past ten years, and many of these are capacity-constrained airports. There are 240 compatible airports (destinations and alternates) with the potential for that number to rise to 400 in time.

Not only does the A380 fly to 19 of the world's 20 busiest international airports (Istanbul being the one current exception), but it has also proved capable of servicing networks too, not just the major hubs. Many of these are essential gateways to massive centres of commerce, industry and population.

The aircraft is seen as a major contributor towards airport efficiency at several of these airports. At Frankfurt, for example, the A380 accounts for 21% of all weekly seats and 13% of all weekly movements at the airport. Similar figures are seen in the United Kingdom when looking at a combination of Heathrow and Gatwick – 18% of all weekly seats and 11% of all weekly movements across both airports. Combined, these two airports see more than 400 A380 movements in a single week.

Today, there are 55 so-called Aviation Mega-Cities (defined as cities with more than 10,000 daily international long-haul passengers) that together deal with more than 90% of the

LEFT Asiana Airlines operates six A380s from its hub at Incheon International Airport. *(Airbus)*

BELOW Airbus flew a test aircraft to Washington for airport trials and the city is now served by regular A380 services from Dubai (Emirates), London (British Airways) and Paris (Air France). *(Airbus)*

ABOVE China Southern's A380s fly to international cities including Guangzhou, Los Angeles, Shenzen and Beijing. (Airbus)

AIRBUS LIST PRICES

2017 average list prices	US$m	GBPm
A318	75.9	58.44
A319	90.5	69.69
A320	99.0	76.23
A321	116.0	89.32
A319 neo*	99.5	76.62
A320 neo	108.4	83.47
A321 neo	127.0	97.79
A330-200	233.8	180.03
A330-800 neo	254.8	196.20
A330-200 Freighter	237.9	183.18
A330-300	259.0	199.43
A330-900 neo	290.6	223.76
A350-800	275.1	211.83
A350-900	311.2	239.62
A350-1000	359.3	276.66
A380-800	436.9	336.41

* 'neo' stands for new engine option
Conversion based on US$/GBP exchange rate of US$1 = GBP 0.77

world's long-haul traffic. More than a million passengers move daily to, from or via one of the Mega-Cities and the A380 currently serves 38 of these.

Many of these big city airports are under enormous capacity and environmental strain. Significant expansion at London's Heathrow, for example, will be impossible without the construction of a third runway and, at the time of writing, it could be several years away before it becomes a reality.

By 2024 the number of Mega-Cities is expected to increase to 75 and that figure will rise to a staggering 93 by 2035, driven predominantly by expanding urbanisation and the rapid growth of emerging markets. As these cities exert more dominance on the long-haul market, the concentration of long-haul traffic between them will correspondingly expand. It is these lucrative routes, with their already-dense traffic and congested airports that are, and will continue to be, the primary home and source of growth for the A380.

RIGHT Air France currently have ten A380 aircraft in service. (Engine Alliance)

If the forecasts are right, then the prospects for the A380 may be rather brighter than either Boeing or Airbus's critics would like to think.

Challenges

Building the world's largest airliner capable of offering the required capacity and range requirements but with a 15–20% cost saving per seat mile over the Boeing 747 was not without difficulties.

Initial studies quickly confirmed that existing technologies would not allow key objectives to be met and hence significant innovation would be required in virtually all areas of design, including aerodynamics, structures, systems, design processes and, ultimately, in manufacturing.

One of the key challenges was to ensure the aircraft could operate using existing airport infrastructure. It had to be able to land and take off from existing runways, use existing ground support infrastructure and, ideally, not require significant investment from airports to accommodate its operation.

Establishing production facilities across Europe and a global supply chain added to the mix, not to mention the need for a multimodal transport and logistics system designed to get the various major components to the FAL in Toulouse.

Once production was up and running, bottlenecks were encountered in the definition, manufacturing and installation of the A380's

complex cabin wiring. The system has more than 330 miles of wiring and over 40,000 connectors in each aircraft and problems started because two incompatible versions of computer-aided design software were used. When it came to fitting the electrical harnesses in the forward and aft fuselage sections, many didn't connect with one another.

This situation, combined with the high level of aircraft customisation to meet customer specifications, would lead to a build-up of delivery delays.

In June 2006, Airbus outlined a series of actions dealing with the situation, including new processes for the outfitting of A380 fuselage sections and a revised schedule of their transfer

ABOVE An A380 on display at the Singapore Air Show in 2016. *(Airbus)*

LEFT The list price of an individual A380 is some £336 million. *(Author)*

ABOVE Air France had the first of its A380 fleet delivered in October 2009. *(Airbus)*

Airbus believes the A380 is an essential part of the solution to sustainable growth, doing more with less – alleviating traffic congestion at busy airports by transporting more passengers with fewer flights, more efficiently and at much lower cost. This remarkable aircraft's most salient features can best be summed up in five key areas, all of which are dealt with in further detail in later chapters.

Performance

Despite its size and weight, the A380 delivers some astonishing performance figures, thanks largely to its state-of-the-art engines and remarkable wing design. Compared with the Boeing 747, the A380 offers 900nm more range, is capable of using runways that are 17% shorter on take-off and 11% shorter on landing. The A380 has a higher initial cruise altitude, can offer the same cruise Mach number and has a 20kt lower approach speed (the same as an A320).

BELOW The first A380 in the British Airways fleet arrived at Heathrow in early July 2013 – it was the first to be owned by a UK airline. *(Author)*

to the FAL. The recovery process would take some time to put the A380 output back on track, but its initial results were confirmed with Airbus's delivery of 12 aircraft to customers during 2008.

A380 features

The double-deck A380 is the world's largest commercial aircraft flying today, operating some of the world's longest commercial routes.

Economics

The A380's systems are two generations ahead of the Boeing 747, resulting in them being lighter in weight and having significantly lower maintenance costs. Composite materials

account for 25% of the aircraft's structural weight, yielding a 15-tonne weight saving. This, together with the latest-generation engines from Rolls-Royce and Engine Alliance mean the A380 has the lowest cost per seat of any wide-body aircraft. From a marketing perspective, the A380 has proved to be a remarkable passenger magnet and engaged customers tend to mean higher load factors and higher profits for airlines.

Innovation

Airbus has truly leveraged the latest technology, employed some of the most advanced materials (in vast quantities) in the build process and ensured the aircraft was certified to the very latest standards. Major innovations include the aircraft's remarkable wings, complex fuel system, state-of-the-art landing gear and global customer support technology, not to mention the new-generation flight deck.

Passenger comfort

The A380 carries between 379 and 615 passengers in a variety of configurations on routes up to 8,200nm (15,200km). From a customer perspective, the aircraft is the most spacious airliner ever conceived. With

two decks, wider seats, broader aisles and more floor space, the aircraft can be customised by airlines to meet new cabin trends and passenger expectations. Cabin offerings range from a comfortable 11-abreast economy section with 18in-wide seats, up to a private three-room suite for a luxurious first-class experience.

Environmental credentials

With the lowest fuel burn per seat, the A380 allows airlines to substantially reduce their environmental footprint in terms of CO_2 emissions. The aircraft also delivers on

ABOVE Asiana Airlines have been operating the A380 since 2014. *(Airbus)*

LEFT Korean Air's first A380 entered service in 2011 – their aircraft have the fewest number of seats (407) of any operator. *(Airbus)*

FACT SHEET

- Each A380 consists of around 4 million individual components with 2.5 million part numbers produced by 1,500 companies from 30 countries around the world.
- Emirates completed the world's longest non-stop flight on an A380 between Dubai and Auckland on 2 March 2016 after traversing 14,200km. It took 17 hours and 15 minutes.
- During take-off the wing will flex upwards by over 4m.
- The A380 wing is the largest produced for a civil airliner. The weight of the external paint is 531kg.
- The 280,000lb of take-off thrust across the wing is the horsepower equivalent of around 2,500 family cars (at 110hp each).
- Today the A380 fleet makes over 300 flights per day and carries more than 3 million passengers per month.
- The Wright Brothers' first flight was shorter than the A380's wingspan.
- There are more than 330 miles of cable wired throughout the aircraft.
- The aircraft is 15 tonnes lighter than it would be if made entirely of metal.
- The air in the cabin is changed every 2 minutes.
- Some 19,000 bolts are inserted inside the fuselage to attach each of the three main sections.
- The span of the horizontal stabiliser is 30.4m; this is just a bit less than the wingspan of the wings of the A320 at 34.9m.
- The volume of the three decks (including the cargo/baggage hold) is 1,570m^3, enough space for 35 million ping-pong balls.
- The two passenger decks are the same size as three tennis courts.
- The engine's 2.95m-diameter fan blades suck in over 1.25 tons of air every second.
- Should it be necessary, the aircraft carrying 853 passengers may be evacuated in only 78 seconds through its 16 doors.

BELOW A comparison of the Boeing 747-400 and Airbus A380-800.
(Roy Scorer)

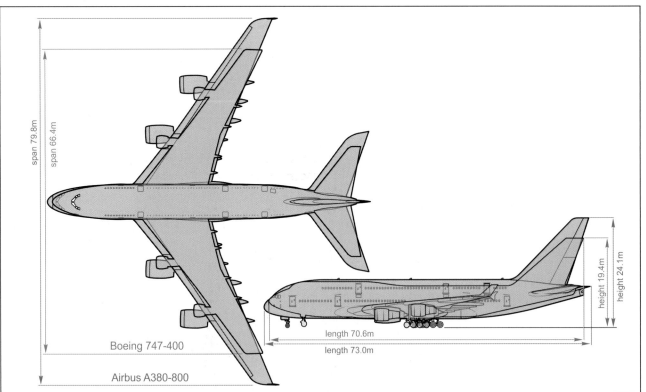

span 79.8m

span 66.4m

height 19.4m

height 24.1m

length 70.6m

length 73.0m

Boeing 747-400

Airbus A380-800

LEFT An A380 prepares to leave the final assembly line – the combined floor space of the two decks is 50 per cent greater than that of the Boeing 747. (*Airbus*)

reduced noise, and is set to remain the quietest long-haul aircraft for the foreseeable future, generating only half the noise on departure as the Boeing 747, and three to four times less noise on landing – while carrying 60% more passengers.

Anatomy of the A380

The A380 is considered a Very Long Range (VLR), subsonic civil transport aircraft. The design combines the in-service experience gained from Airbus A330 and A340 aircraft combined with new technology developed specifically for the A380 programme.

The general arrangement is a four-engine configuration with rearward swept low wing and a conventional tail. The basic model is the A380-800 long-range passenger model. The aircraft represents the continuation of a long line of technologically advanced Airbus aircraft and introduces a step-change in performance, comfort standards, environmental friendliness and efficiency.

The key dimensions are that it is 72.7m long, 24.1m high and 79.8m wide. Put another way,

TECHNICAL SPECIFICATIONS

Overall length	72.72m		Engines	Rolls-Royce Trent 900
Cabin length	49.90m			Engine Alliance GP7200
Fuselage diameter	7.14m			
Maximum cabin width – main deck	6.5m		Engine thrust range	70,000lb
Maximum cabin width – upper deck	5.8m		Usable fuel capacity	323,546 litres
			Pressurised fuselage volume	$2,100m^3$
Wingspan	79.8m		Passenger compartment volume – main deck	$775m^3$
Wing area	$845m^2$			
Wing sweep	33.5°		Passenger compartment volume – upper deck	$530m^3$
Height	24.09m			
Track	14.34m		Cockpit volume	$12m^3$
Wheelbase	31.88m		Usable volume – forward hold	$89.4m^3$
Long-range cruise	Mach 0.85		Usable volume – aft hold	$71.5m^3$
Typical passenger seating	525 in three classes		Usable volume – bulk	$14.3m^3$
Range (w/max. passengers)	8,200nm/15,200km		Water volume – forward	$131m^3$
Maximum take-off weight	560t/575t		Water volume – aft	$107.8m^3$
Maximum landing weight	386t/394t		Water volume – bulk	$17.3m^3$
Maximum zero fuel weight	361t/369t			
Maximum fuel capacity	320,000 litres			

Anatomy of the A380.

(Alex Pang)

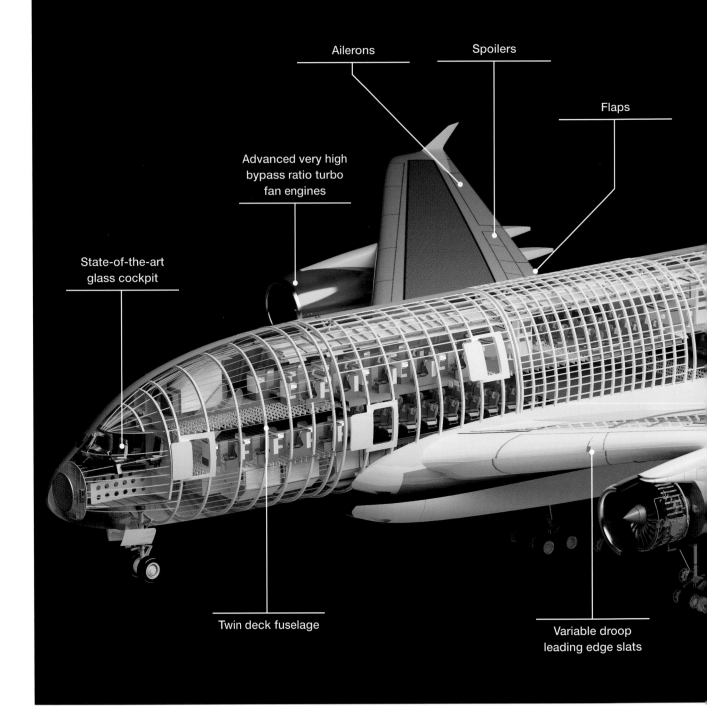

Ailerons

Spoilers

Flaps

Advanced very high
bypass ratio turbo
fan engines

State-of-the-art
glass cockpit

Twin deck fuselage

Variable droop
leading edge slats

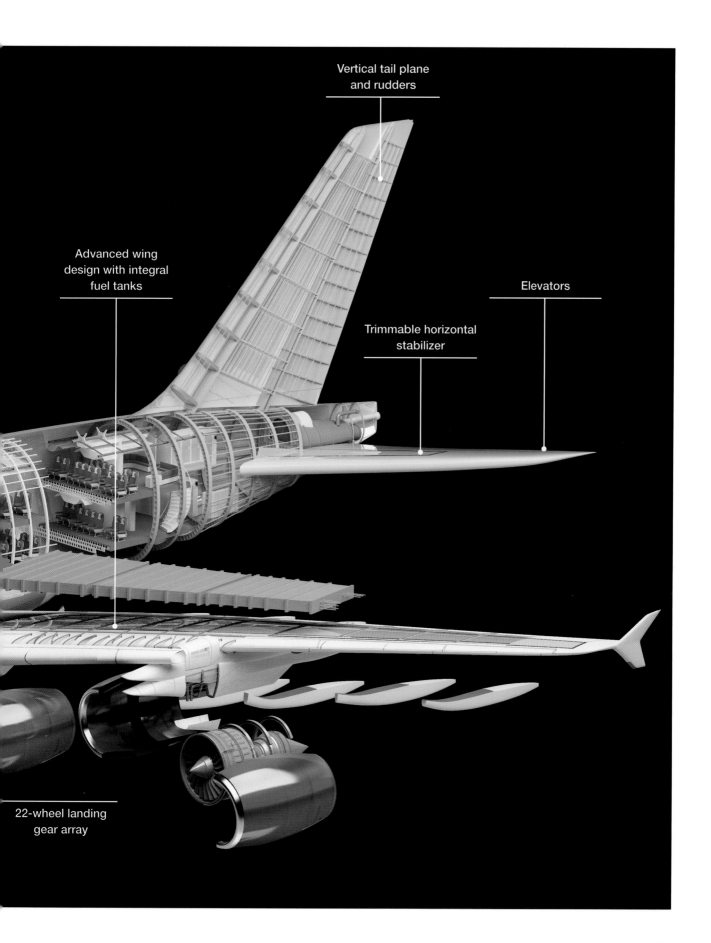

Vertical tail plane
and rudders

Advanced wing
design with integral
fuel tanks

Elevators

Trimmable horizontal
stabilizer

22-wheel landing
gear array

Singapore Airlines (SIA) put its first Airbus A380 into commercial service, commencing with regular daily flights between Singapore and Sydney. The airline's 471-seat A380s would carry 30% more passengers than its 370-seat 747-400s and the launch attracted global media attention.

The entry into service was not without challenges; with a demanding flight schedule and only the single A380 delivered that year, the airline had no easy backup solution should a flight have to be cancelled.

To its credit, Airbus was described as 'behaving with an airline mindset' during preparation for the A380's service entry, working through a multi-point plan to ensure both the A380 and SIA were service ready. The plan comprised an operational readiness campaign and validation of the aircraft under airline conditions, training the airline's personnel, ensuring that the required spares were in place and finally a fully integrated real-time support network was ready across the globe that would cosset the aircraft during early operations.

In the lead-up to the launch, Airbus had benefited from ten months of proving the aircraft for service, and this enabled it to generate an unprecedented number of flying hours for an aircraft ahead of service entry. A full team of Airbus engineers were

ABOVE No other commercial airliner has the distinctive and imposing shape of the A380. *(Lufthansa)*

the plane is twice as long as a blue whale, the tail is as high as five giraffes standing on top of one another and the combined floor space of the two decks is 50% greater than that of the previous record holder, Boeing's 747.

Entry into service

The first A380 flight took place in Toulouse on 27 April 2005 and by October 2007

RIGHT The A380 on display at the Paris Air Show at Le Bourget Airport in France. *(Airbus)*

positioned in Singapore to support early operations and assist with new systems on the aircraft. Time was also spent ensuring turnround times in Sydney could be met during route-proving and long-haul campaigns to validate the A380's 90-minute turnround target.

The next two customers to receive the A380 were Emirates and Qantas with deliveries that began the following summer.

ABOVE Qantas was an early adopter of the A380 and to date has received 12 of its initial order of 20 aircraft. *(Airbus)*

AIRLINE CUSTOMERS

Airline	Aircraft in service*	Destinations*	First service
Air France	10	11	20 November 2009
Asiana Airlines	6	5	13 June 2014
British Airways	12	9	2 August 2013
China Southern	5	8	17 October 2011
Emirates	94	46	1 August 2008
Etihad	8	6	27 December 2014
Korean Air	10	6	17 June 2011
Lufthansa	14	12	6 June 2010
Malaysia Airlines	6	2	1 July 2012
Qantas	12	6	20 October 2008
Qatar Airways	7	6	10 October 2014
Singapore Airlines	19	16	25 October 2007
Thai Airways	6	7	6 October 2012

* Based on July 2017 information

Firm orders	317
Deliveries	209
Order backlog	108

Orders are pending from some major carriers including Virgin Atlantic and All Nippon Airways.

To put the aircraft's use into perspective, by April 2017, the global fleet of A380s had completed more than 450,000 revenue flights, amassed more than 3.8 million flight hours and carried in excess of 170 million passengers around the world.

An A380 from Etihad cruises effortlessly at 36,000ft. *(Airbus)*

CHAPTER 2

Innovation

OPPOSITE The aircraft's remarkable landing gear is clearly visible as this British Airways A380 takes off. *(Airbus)*

RIGHT The A380 has pushed aviation boundaries with the sheer number of innovations and technological advances. (Author)

Introduction

Once market interest had been established, it was evident that the design and engineering challenges for the A380 would be substantial. Since its inception, Airbus has played a pioneering role in the international air transport industry's evolution and the A380 would present the ideal platform from which Airbus could successfully leverage and create innovative solutions for this truly unique aircraft.

With any new aircraft, emphasis is always based on improving economic efficiency and environmental performance, but today's commercial jets are the result of more than 50 years of optimisation of what is essentially the same concept, hence significant improvements are hard to realise.

Simply scaling up the A380 based on existing technologies was never going to be sufficient, especially when the additional requirements of more cabin space per passenger, additional range and significantly lower noise were taken into consideration. There was a further requirement for the A380 to maximise the efficiency of existing airport infrastructure – by suitably adapting the A380 at an early stage of development, Airbus were able to either reduce or defer the need for airports to invest in the duplication of existing infrastructure.

Adopting an innovative approach in the design, development and testing played a key role, as did the use of advanced materials in key components, thereby saving weight and improving efficiency. Other major innovations include the aircraft's remarkable wings, complex fuel system, state-of-the-art landing gear and global customer support technology. Another major innovation came in the way of a new-generation flight deck – an amazing step forward in design and development but still capable of sharing a large degree of commonality in systems, procedures and maintainability with the wider Airbus family of aircraft. This means pilots do not need extensive training to transfer from one aircraft type to another, increasing their productivity and reducing training costs. There is an in-depth look at the A380 cockpit in Chapter 5.

With everything from new flight control architecture to state-of-the-art aerodynamics, the A380 today benefits from lower fuel-burn, higher levels of reliability and lower maintenance costs. Importantly, there has also been continuous innovation with the A380 since its entry into service, with the likes of the Brake to Vacate (BTV) system introduced

BELOW Aircraft MSN 152 at Station 30 in Toulouse. (Airbus)

in 2008, the pilot head-up display (HUD) in 2009, improvements to the instrument landing system (ILS) in 2010, weight reductions in early 2012 and a revamped cabin design in 2017 to mention but a few of the amazing developments brought to the market by Airbus for the A380.

Ultimately, the sheer number of advanced technology-manufacturing techniques, components and capabilities introduced and integrated in one aircraft makes the A380 a major advance in aviation innovation and this chapter explores many of the key elements to show just how Airbus pushed the boundaries to innovate, develop and maximise the potential of the A380.

Testing and development

Airbus and the launch airlines spent four years preparing for the giant's introduction into commercial service. Airbus wanted to avoid a repeat of the mistakes it encountered with the introduction of the A340-600 and ensure that the A380

ABOVE Airbus technical crews install the aircraft's state-of-the-art cockpit on the final assembly line. *(Author)*

BELOW The A380 has continued with innovations since its entry into service in 2007. *(Author)*

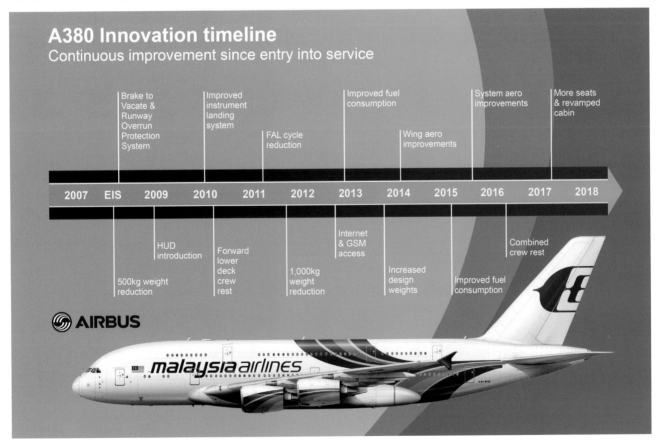

A380 Innovation timeline
Continuous improvement since entry into service

	Brake to Vacate & Runway Overrun Protection System	Improved instrument landing system		Improved fuel consumption		System aero improvements	More seats & revamped cabin
			FAL cycle reduction		Wing aero improvements		

2007	EIS	2009	2010	2011	2012	2013	2014	2015	2016	2017	2018

		HUD introduction	Forward lower deck crew rest			Internet & GSM access	Increased design weights		Improved fuel consumption	Combined crew rest	
	500kg weight reduction				1,000kg weight reduction						

AIRBUS

malaysia airlines

ABOVE Malaysia Airlines' new pilgrimage charter airline will commence operations in late 2018 and will utilise the national carrier's fleet of six Airbus A380s. *(Airbus)*

BELOW The A380's innovative central wing box was the first to be made of carbon fibre reinforced plastic. *(Airbus)*

exhibited the reliability of a mature airliner as soon as it took to the skies. Similarly, the airlines had to gear up for operations with the world's largest airliner.

Airbus set a dispatch reliability target of 99%, which it wanted to achieve from entry into service and planned a comprehensive test programme to determine how the aircraft would behave in operation. Cold weather tests were carried out in Iqualit, Canada, high-altitude tests were conducted in Medellín, Colombia, while a series of hot weather tests were completed in Al Ain, UAE.

Considerable time was spent testing the aircraft's fuel system by setting up fuel test rigs in the UK to trial the fuel management computer software, the gauging and how the fully integrated system worked.

Another key area in the A380's development focused on increasing redundancy to enable the release of the aircraft by applying the exact same methodology to the cabin environment as the one we have for airworthiness systems. An example of this is a failure on the entertainment system or a malfunctioning toilet – either of which could have a potentially high commercial impact to the airline.

Given the specific context of A380 operations – high capacity, long haul and with no substitute aircraft available – Airbus also set about creating an enhanced support structure to address the time taken to rectify an in-service problem.

Advanced materials

The Airbus A380 has attracted kudos for its ground-breaking structural composite airframe design and use of some of the latest advances in assembly and materials. The design incorporates as much as 25% composite material, particularly in the centre wing box's primary structure, wing ribs and rear fuselage section.

This makes the A380 the first commercial airliner to have a central wing box made of carbon fibre reinforced plastic (CFRP). This innovative structure alone saves 1.5 tonnes of weight, while the overall weight saving from the use of advanced materials is estimated to be between 10 and 15 tonnes.

Other notable achievements include the use of advanced weldable aluminium alloys for the fuselage, enabling the widespread use of laser beam welding manufacturing techniques, eliminating rows of rivets and resulting in a lighter, stronger structure.

The A380 also uses Glare™ (glass laminate aluminium reinforced epoxy) material in the pressurised fuselage's upper and lateral shells. Glare™ is a laminate incorporating alternate

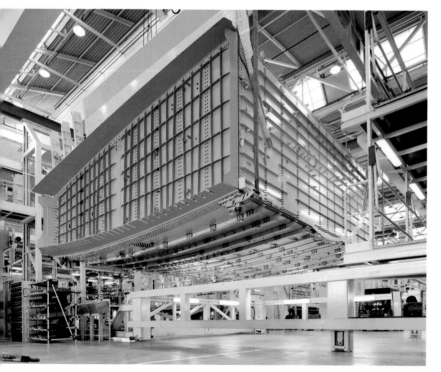

layers of aluminium alloy and glass fibre reinforced adhesive, with its properties optimised by adjusting the number of plies and the orientation of the glass tapes. This offers a significant reduction in weight and provides advanced fatigue and damage resistance characteristics.

Composite materials are vitally important to the aviation industry because they provide structural strength comparable to metallic alloys but at a lighter weight, which in turn means significant fuel savings, better performance and a much-improved bottom line for airlines. These weight savings enable the A380 to offer the lowest 'cost-per-seat' of any wide-body aircraft, some 15% lower than its nearest competitor.

Components and structures made of composite materials comprise a quarter of the A380 by weight, which compares with 10% in the A320, 16% in the A340 and about 3% in the original A300. Airbus is continuing the growing trend and its latest aircraft, the A350, has some 53%.

The widespread increase in composite usage has brought a series of concerns and changes in the aviation industry, particularly in terms of maintenance, repair and overhaul (MRO). Maintenance requirements of composite materials are very different from those of metals; most MRO companies do not have much experience

COMPOSITES

Composites are made from two or more constituent materials with significantly different physical or chemical properties that, when combined, produce a material with characteristics different from the individual components. The individual components remain separate and distinct within the finished structure. Composites offer benefits over traditional materials to the aviation sector including improved strength and reduced weight.

of maintaining composite structures and although there's a certain degree of standardisation for the repair and maintenance of metals in aircraft, the same is not yet true for composites.

Wings

As with any aircraft, the wings are the crucial element in meeting the required performance targets; the wing has to generate sufficient lift while keeping the weight and drag to a minimum in order to minimise fuel-burn and maximise range. As the wings also act as the main fuel tank of the aircraft, the design team

BELOW Those gigantic wings house 10 separate fuel tanks and generate sufficient lift to get the A380 off the ground. *(Airbus)*

had to ensure they would be large enough to hold sufficient fuel for the flight but also that there was adequate spare capacity to allow for future, longer-range developments of the aircraft.

The Airbus facility at Broughton is where the A380's remarkable wings are manufactured (see Chapter 3 for more details). The development team faced a variety of technical challenges in designing them, but used advanced technology and innovation to meet the required performance goals.

The high-capacity, 575 tonnes take-off weight and long-range requirements meant a very large wing would be needed to lift the aircraft, but it was obvious constraints – for instance, if it was too big, the wing would trigger major compatibility problems at airports

in terms of manoeuvring and stand space. To deal with this, geometric constraints were placed on the wing to ensure that the aircraft would have minimal impact on airports. Consideration also had to be given to passenger evacuation requirements, drag, weight cost and systems installation needs.

Significant developments in the wing design included:

- Lightweight 'trussed' ribs, part of the internal wing skeleton, were developed for the leading edge of the wing in partnership with an external software company, which saved several hundreds of kilograms in weight.
- The box beam structures that attach the trailing edge flaps to the main structure of the wing were changed to a predominantly CFRP design, achieving significant weight savings.
- A detailed investigation of the main wing ribs led to the decision to make about half their number in CFRP for additional weight saving – the first such innovation for a large civil aircraft.

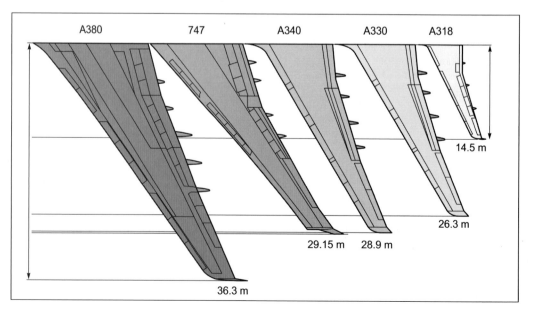

RIGHT The A380's wing dwarfs everything else, including the Boeing 747 and Airbus A340. *(Roy Scorer)*

A380   747   A340   A330   A318

14.5 m

26.3 m

29.15 m   28.9 m

36.3 m

- Where it was not effective to introduce such composites, traditional aerospace aluminium alloys were developed in conjunction with material suppliers to optimise their material properties for the A380 application. Combined with design optimisation techniques, this enabled the overall wing weight to be reduced by several tonnes.
- The A380 was also the first to have a smoothly contoured wing cross-section – the wings of other commercial airliners are partitioned span-wise into sections, and this flowing, continuous cross-section on the super jumbo helps to optimise aerodynamic efficiency.
- Thermoplastics are used in the leading edges of the slats. The hybrid fibre metal laminate material Glare™ is used on the stabilisers' leading edges. It is lighter and has better corrosion and impact resistance than conventional aluminium alloys used in aviation.
- Also like the A320, the A380 uses a combined load alleviation function (LAF). When the aircraft executes a manoeuvre the system is designed to deflect the wing movable surfaces to minimise the loads. In a similar fashion the controls will also deploy when the aircraft encounters turbulence, again with the aim of reducing loads on the wing.
- The integration of wingtip devices similar to those found on the A310 and A320 to reduce induced drag, increase fuel efficiency and performance.

The A380 has also benefited from improved manufacturing techniques, not only to optimise the build process but also to save weight – particularly in the wings. The metallic sheets (the 'skins') that make up the top and bottom wing surfaces account for around a quarter of the wing weight and needed careful optimisation. As with most aircraft, the thickness of these skins is not uniform and varies considerably due to the range of loads which must be catered for, including

ABOVE Thermoplastics are used in the leading edges of the slats. (Author)

BELOW More than 100 wing design concepts were generated and carefully analysed before a decision was taken to move into production. (Author)

Airbus A380-800. *(Mike Badrocke)*

1 Radome
2 Weather radar antenna
3 Antenna mounting structure
4 Dual. ILS antennae
5 Front pressure bulkhead
6 Nose undercarriage wheel bay
7 Cockpit pressure floor
8 Rudder pedals
9 Side console with sidestick controller
10 Instrument panel with ten full colour multi-function displays
11 Windscreen wipers
12 Electrically heated windscreen panels
13 Overhead systems switch panel
14 Two-pilot cockpit with central Observer's seat
15 Cockpit bulkhead
16 Maintenance station
17 Folding supernumerary crew seats, port and starboard
18 Main avionics equipment bay
19 Nose undercarriage pivot mounting
20 Nosewheel leg doors
21 Leg mounted taxying lights
22 Twin nosewheels, forward retracting
23 Hydraulic nosewheel steering
24 Forward main entry door, all doors outward opening
25 Crew toilet
26 Closet
27 Crew rest compartment
28 Upper avionics equipment bay
29 Forward staircase
30 Lower deck toilet compartment
31 Fuselage lower lobe structure with welded skin/stringer panels
32 First class passenger cabin, 22-seats, six-abreast
33 Upper deck toilet compartment
34 Overhead baggage lockers
35 Cabin roof trim/lighting panels
36 Passenger service units
37 Business class passenger cabin, 96 seats, six-abreast
38 Curtained cabin divider Main deck galley compartment
39 Wing and engine inspection lights
40 Forward cargo hold, capacity 20 x LD3 containers or
41 7 x 88in or 96in x 125in pallets, door on starboard side
42 Conditioned air mixing and distribution units
43 Wing centre box carry-through structure with CFRP skins and web panels, dry bay on 800 series aircraft
44 Upper deck forward door, port and starboard
45 Upper deck window panels
46 Upper deck galley compartment
47 Forward service trolley lift
48 Cabin wall trim paneling
49 Starboard wing inboard fuel tank
50 Starboard mid tank, total usable fuel capacity 69,356 Imp gal (315,292-lit, 83,296 US gal)
51 Inboard drooped leading edge, lowered
52 Starboard thrust reverser, open
53 Starboard engine nacelles

54 Nacelle pylons
55 Central leading edge slats, extended
56 Pressure refuelling/defuelling connectors
57 Slat torque shaft and rack—and-pinion drive mechanism
58 Wing skin panelling
59 Wing stringers
60 Starboard feed tank
61 Fuel feed and vent piping
62 Surge tank
63 Outer fuel tank
64 Outboard leading edge slats, extended
65 Wing tip vent tank
66 Starboard navigation (green) and strobe (white) lights
67 Starboard winglet
68 Obstruction light
69 Static dischargers
70 Starboard three-segment aileron
71 Aileron hydraulic actuators
72 Outboard two-segment single-slotted flap, extended
73 Flap aluminium alloy structure with honeycomb trailing edge
74 Outboard spoiler panels (6)
75 Flap carriages and hinge links
76 Flap operating links, torque shaft driven
77 Twin anti-collision beacons
78 Fuselage frame and stringer structure
79 Floor beam structure above wing box centre section
80 Forward end of aft T-section cargo hold, capacity 16 x LD3 containers or 6 x LD3 containers and 3 pallets
81 Starboard wing-mounted main undercarriage, stowed position
82 Lower deck overwing door panel, port and starboard
83 Cabin wall insulation
84 Lower deck overhead baggage lockers
85 Starboard fuselage-mounted main undercarriage, stowed position
86 Aft end of Business class cabin
87 Curtained cabin divider
88 ADF antennae

89 Upper deck Tourist-class seating, eight-abreast
90 Main deck Tourist class seating, ten-abreast, total of 437 Tourist class seats
91 Main deck window panels
92 Escape chute stowage, all upper deck door positions
93 Upper deck mid doors, port and starboard
94 Fuselage 'Glare' upper skin panels
95 Aft cargo hold door
96 Main deck cabin wall trim paneling
97 Upper deck aft door, port and starboard
98 Cabin attendant's folding seat, typical
99 Aft upper deck galley unit, crew rest area on port side
100 Aft service trolley lift
101 Aft staircase
102 Rear pressure bulkhead, aluminium alloy frame and CFRP dome structure
103 Machined fin support frames
104 Fin root bolted attachment joints
105 CFRP fin leading edge structure
106 Starboard trimming tail plane

107 Tail plane integral trimming fuel tank
108 Tailplane vent tank, starboard side only
109 Starboard outboard elevator panel
110 Fin CFRP skin panels
111 Fin two-spar and rib all-CFRP torsion box structure
112 Upper rudder segment
113 Rudder hydraulic actuators
114 Lower rudder segment
115 Rudder CFRP rib and skin structure

116 Tailplane mounting bulkhead
117 Tailplane pivot mountings, port and starboard
118 APU bay fireproof bulkhead
119 APU intake
120 PW980A auxiliary power unit (APU)
121 Rear position light
122 APU exhaust
123 Port inboard elevator
124 Elevator hydraulic actuators
125 Port outboard elevator segment
126 Elevator CFRP rib and skin structure
127 Static dischargers
128 Aluminium alloy tailplane tip fairing
129 Tailplane two-spar and rib all-CFRP torsion box structure
130 Fin 'logo' light
131 Tailplane sliding root seal
132 Tailplane screw jack trim actuator, hydraulic motor driven
133 Fuselage tailcone frame and stringer structure
134 Main deck aft door, port and starboard

46

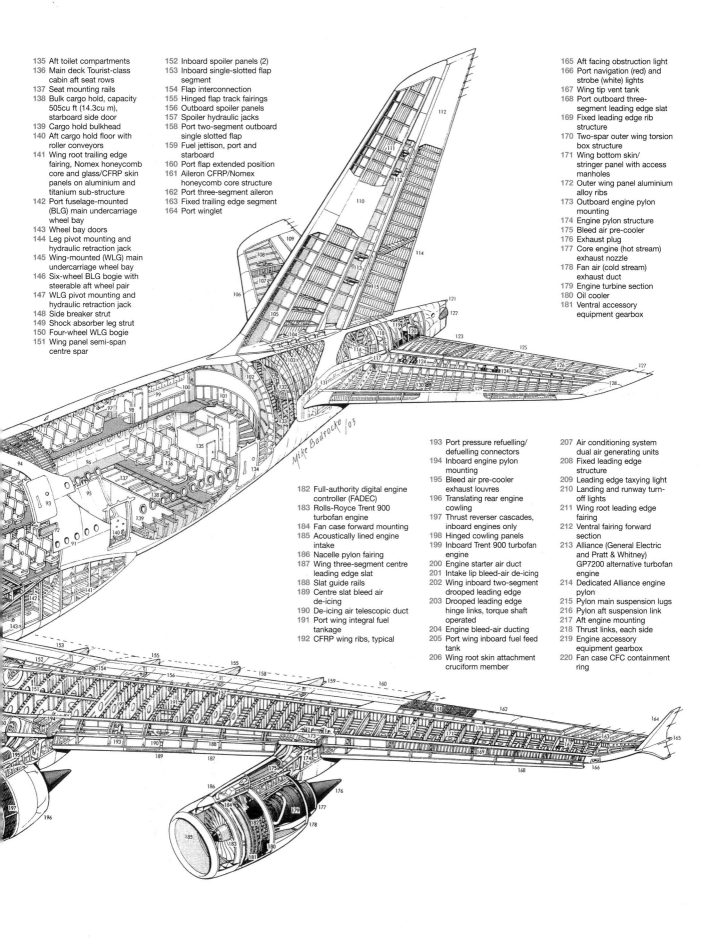

135 Aft toilet compartments
136 Main deck Tourist-class cabin aft seat rows
137 Seat mounting rails
138 Bulk cargo hold, capacity 505cu ft (14.3cu m), starboard side door
139 Cargo hold bulkhead
140 Aft cargo hold floor with roller conveyors
141 Wing root trailing edge fairing, Nomex honeycomb core and glass/CFRP skin panels on aluminium and titanium sub-structure
142 Port fuselage-mounted (BLG) main undercarriage wheel bay
143 Wheel bay doors
144 Leg pivot mounting and hydraulic retraction jack
145 Wing-mounted (WLG) main undercarriage wheel bay
146 Six-wheel BLG bogie with steerable aft wheel pair
147 WLG pivot mounting and hydraulic retraction jack
148 Side breaker strut
149 Shock absorber leg strut
150 Four-wheel WLG bogie
151 Wing panel semi-span centre spar

152 Inboard spoiler panels (2)
153 Inboard single-slotted flap segment
154 Flap interconnection
155 Hinged flap track fairings
156 Outboard spoiler panels
157 Spoiler hydraulic jacks
158 Port two-segment outboard single slotted flap
159 Fuel jettison, port and starboard
160 Port flap extended position
161 Aileron CFRP/Nomex honeycomb core structure
162 Port three-segment aileron
163 Fixed trailing edge segment
164 Port winglet

165 Aft facing obstruction light
166 Port navigation (red) and strobe (white) lights
167 Wing tip vent tank
168 Port outboard three-segment leading edge slat
169 Fixed leading edge rib structure
170 Two-spar outer wing torsion box structure
171 Wing bottom skin/ stringer panel with access manholes
172 Outer wing panel aluminium alloy ribs
173 Outboard engine pylon mounting
174 Engine pylon structure
175 Bleed air pre-cooler
176 Exhaust plug
177 Core engine (hot stream) exhaust nozzle
178 Fan air (cold stream) exhaust duct
179 Engine turbine section
180 Oil cooler
181 Ventral accessory equipment gearbox

182 Full-authority digital engine controller (FADEC)
183 Rolls-Royce Trent 900 turbofan engine
184 Fan case forward mounting
185 Acoustically lined engine intake
186 Nacelle pylon fairing
187 Wing three-segment centre leading edge slat
188 Slat guide rails
189 Centre slat bleed air de-icing
190 De-icing air telescopic duct
191 Port wing integral fuel tankage
192 CFRP wing ribs, typical

193 Port pressure refuelling/ defuelling connectors
194 Inboard engine pylon mounting
195 Bleed air pre-cooler exhaust louvres
196 Translating rear engine cowling
197 Thrust reverser cascades, inboard engines only
198 Hinged cowling panels
199 Inboard Trent 900 turbofan engine
200 Engine starter air duct
201 Intake lip bleed-air de-icing
202 Wing inboard two-segment drooped leading edge
203 Drooped leading edge hinge links, torque shaft operated
204 Engine bleed-air ducting
205 Port wing inboard fuel feed tank
206 Wing root skin attachment cruciform member

207 Air conditioning system dual air generating units
208 Fixed leading edge structure
209 Leading edge taxying light
210 Landing and runway turn-off lights
211 Wing root leading edge fairing
212 Ventral fairing forward section
213 Alliance (General Electric and Pratt & Whitney) GP7200 alternative turbofan engine
214 Dedicated Alliance engine pylon
215 Pylon main suspension lugs
216 Pylon aft suspension link
217 Aft engine mounting
218 Thrust links, each side
219 Engine accessory equipment gearbox
220 Fan case CFC containment ring

Mike Badrocke/'03

wing-bending loads and those created by engine, flap support systems and landing gear attachments.

Modern machining methods certainly get close to achieving the complex three-dimensional geometry required by the structural engineers, but the process has its limitations, which result in some unnecessary material being left on the skins. Airbus went one step further to remove this weight penalty by using a patented machining method of milling longitudinal strips of varying heights into the raw material billet, resulting ultimately in significant weight savings and associated manufacturing benefits.

The Airbus design team made extensive use of knowledge-based engineering (KBE) techniques to achieve key performance targets. KBE is the application of knowledge-based systems technology to the domain of manufacturing design and production. The design process is inherently a knowledge-intensive activity, so a great deal of the emphasis for KBE is on the use of knowledge-based technology to support computer-aided design (CAD); however, knowledge-based techniques (e.g. knowledge management) can be applied to the entire product lifecycle.

The advantages of KBE for Airbus included improved integration and collaboration by the design team by using a standardised knowledge model across different systems

and applications. KBE's scope includes design, analysis, manufacturing and support. KBE enabled a significant reduction in time needed to generate the production and analysis of a specific wing geometry and structural layout. It also enabled concurrent working on a common set of data and the ability for the specialist departments to plug in their own design tools at a much earlier stage of the design process, providing improvements in quality and accuracy of results. KBE was applied and aided in a variety of areas, such as generating a three-dimensional wing surface from the two-dimensional aerofoil sections produced by the aerodynamicists in a matter of minutes. Similar time reductions were also achieved in fuel tank modelling, structural sizing and weight estimation.

Airbus also ensured that its aerodynamicists could devote their time to developing the wing rather than spend time laboriously processing the vast quantities of data generated by the aerodynamic design process. The manufacturer provided for a new data-processing suite, which allowed a more efficient transfer of aerodynamic data (both predicted and wind tunnel-generated). Design times were shortened further by improving wind tunnel model manufacture time.

This helped to speed up the time taken from generating initial computer predictions to receiving wind tunnel results and was primarily achieved by using stereolithography, an early form of 3D printing that continues to be one of the most widely used rapid prototyping technologies for plastic models. This laser-based technology involves a UV-sensitive liquid resin and a UV laser beam which scans the surface of the resin and selectively hardens the material corresponding to a cross-section of the product, building the 3D part from the bottom to the top. Using geometric data taken directly from the aerodynamic prediction tools, a laser was used to create the final wind tunnel component directly by solidifying a resin-based material.

With more time for design, it was possible to explore a large number of wing design concepts before having to make a final selection. In fact, around 100 concepts were generated and analysed within just six months, leading to the selection of two wings that were then tested against one another in a virtual 'fly-off'. The end result was a significantly lighter wing (by several tonnes) and a better aerodynamic standard than previous products – both key factors in reducing fuel-burn and enabling the A380 to meet set requirements.

Fuel system

It is widely accepted that an aircraft's fuel system has a more profound effect on its performance than any other system and with 11 separate tanks, 21 pumps and 43 valves, the A380's system is one of the most advanced in the world. The size and scale of the A380 also called for a new type of fuel system, owing to the fact that when fully loaded there is some 118 tonnes of fuel being carried in each wing. In fact, the A380 can carry about 320,000 litres of fuel or about 250 metric tonnes, providing it with a range of around 8,000 miles.

Fuel systems are not generally regarded as the most glamorous feature of aircraft functionality but they are an essential one and their implementation and functional characteristics play a critical role in the design, certification and operational aspects of any aircraft. The fuel tanks comprise:

■ **Transfer tanks** – there are seven transfer tanks and these serve two purposes. The first is to store fuel before it is used. The second is to allow easy transfer from tank to tank in order to manage weight distribution. There are three storage tanks in each wing: inner, middle and outer tanks. The trim tank is the seventh transfer tank, located in the horizontal stabiliser – the tail of the aircraft.

■ **Feed tanks** – the basic purpose of a feed tank is to provide fuel directly to the engine. The other tanks transfer the fuel into the feed tanks. Each engine has its own feed tank, but every engine is capable of feeding from others should this be needed. Each feed tank has a collector cell that holds approximately 1 tonne of fuel inside to keep the fuel pumps fully immersed.

■ In addition, there are vent tanks that are used to capture fuel that expands too much and could cause damage to the tank if trapped. The system also has surge tanks that assist in equalising pressure differences.

On the ground, fuel is distributed more centrally, avoiding the outer wing tanks and the additional weight this would unnecessarily place on

BELOW The A380's complex fuel system has 11 separate tanks and is considered one of the most advanced in the world. *(Roy Scorer)*

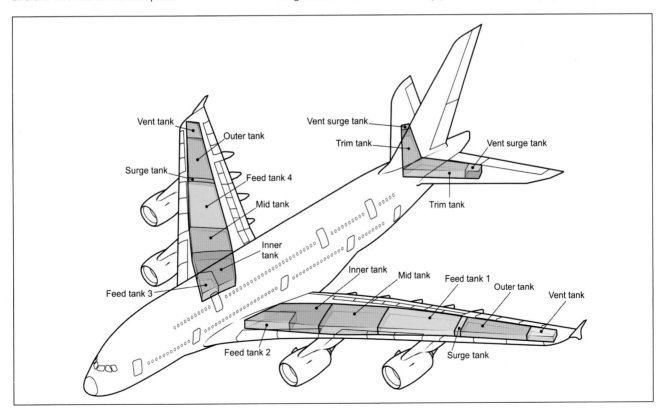

USABLE FUEL (Fuel apecific density: 0.785kg/l)		Outer tanks (each)	Feed tanks ¼ (each)	Mid tanks (each)	Inner tanks (each)	Feed tanks ⅔ (each)	Trim tank	Total
Volume	(litres)	10,520	27,960	36,460	46,140	29,340	23,700	324,540
	(US gal)	2,780	7,390	9,630	12,190	7,750	6,260	85,740
Weight	(kg)	8,260	21,950	28,620	36,220	23,030	18,600	254,760
	(lb)	18,200	48,390	63,100	79,850	50,780	41,020	561,660

the wing structure. After take-off the fuel is redistributed to the outer wing tanks to better spread the weight of the fuel along the length of the wing. This helps to counter the upward flex in the wings during flight.

To rapidly reduce the aircraft's gross weight, fuel can be jettisoned from all the transfer tanks simultaneously at an output rate of approximately 15 tonnes per hour.

Fuel transfer system

Typically, Airbus aircraft pump fuel between the wing tanks and tail tank to maintain the centre of gravity (CG) in the most advantageous place to minimise the drag of the aircraft in cruise. This happens on the A380 too, but here the technique goes one step further. In the A380, fuel is also pumped from the inner wing tanks to the outer wing tanks after take-off and then in the opposite direction before touchdown, which reduces the 'ground–air–ground' fatigue loads on the wing. The combination of these load alleviation techniques saves more than 2.5 tonnes of wing weight.

The purpose of fuel transfers is obviously to provide fuel to the engines (Main Transfers), to reduce the loads on the aircraft structure (Load Alleviation Transfers) and to control the centre of gravity of the aircraft (CG Control Transfers).

■ **Main Transfers** – the quantity of fuel in the feed tanks continuously decreases as a result of engine fuel-burn. Main Transfers are automatic transfers from the other tanks to the feed tanks, and occur in the following sequence:
  ♦ Inner tanks to feed tanks, until empty
  ♦ Mid tanks to feed tanks, until empty
  ♦ Trim tanks to feed tanks, until empty
  ♦ Outer tanks to feed tanks.
■ **Load Alleviation Transfers** – load alleviation transfers occur in flight as follows:
  ♦ After take-off – transfer to the outer tanks, until the outer tanks are full

  ♦ Before landing – transfer from the trim tank, until the trim tank is empty; transfer from the outer tanks, until the outer tanks are half empty.
■ **CG Control Transfers** – these maintain the aircraft's CG forward of the aft certified limit by transferring fuel from the trim tank to the appropriate wing tanks. There are no aft CG transfers, because the CG only has a minor impact on the cruise performance.

Fuel transfers are enabled by two galleries (forward and aft) that pass through all wing tanks (inner, mid, outer and feed tanks). Each wing transfer tank has one or two transfer pumps, each connected to one of the two galleries. A trim pipe connects the trim tank to the galleries. The trim tank is equipped with two trim transfer pumps, each connected to the trim pipe. In normal operation, the forward gallery is for fuel transfers between the wing tanks, while the aft gallery is for fuel transfers between the trim tank and the wing tanks via the trim pipe. The galleries can be connected to each other via two auxiliary refuel valves during refuelling, defuelling and jettison. In the case of a failure of any gallery, the other gallery takes over for alternate fuel transfers using a network of transfer pumps, inlet valves and cross-feed valves.

Once fuel tanks are tested, they are equipped with the systems they need and all the wiring, piping and ducting for the hydraulics that connect the controls and fuel system are installed by 200 workers over a 22-day period.

The A380's Load Alleviation system is a more mature and sensitive system to that used on the Airbus A340-500/600. The main advances come in the form of sharper control software algorithms and better sensors (such as the three sideslip detector vanes on the aircraft's nose – just below the cockpit windscreen) in addition to accelerometers. The sideslip vanes are a first in a commercial transport aircraft.

Fuel quantity and management system (FQMS)

Two FQMS systems are used to perform CG control, fuel transfers between tanks while airborne, fuel flow to engines and the auxiliary power unit, ground operations (refuelling and defuelling) and to control fuel jettison. The system has the ability to move fuel between tanks to optimise the aircraft's CG, reduce wing bending to alleviate structural loads and keep fuel within the acceptable temperature range.

To develop the A380's fuel management system and ensure its ability to safely handle any failure in the system's 21 pumps, 43 valves and other mechanical components, Airbus engineers modelled the system's requirements through simulation to replicate modes of operation on the ground and in flight. This approach enabled the manufacturer to validate requirements months earlier than was previously possible. After running closed-loop simulations of individual operational components, the team integrated them into a complete model and then ran 100,000 simulated flights under varied environmental conditions and aircraft operational scenarios.

These advances in technology helped to cut development time on the Airbus A350 XWB's fuel management system.

Two under-wing refuelling couplings are used when refuelling the aircraft. The A380 uses Jet A and Jet A-1 fuel and a complete refuel can be completed in 45 minutes (with a pressure

ABOVE During flight, fuel is pumped between the wing tanks and tail tank to maintain the centre of gravity, which enables the flight crew to minimise drag and fly as efficiently as possible. *(Airbus)*

LEFT Fuel is pumped into the aircraft via two large hoses connected to the underside of the wing. *(Author)*

ABOVE The refuelling panel on this Emirates A380 shows 94,500kg of fuel has been selected and there is currently 76,500kg of fuel on board. (Author)

BELOW The aircraft's impressive undercarriage comprises two wing landing gears and two body landing gears in addition to the nose landing gear. (Author)

of some 40psi). The FQMS automatically transfers fuel to bring the aircraft's CG within take-off limits. Defuelling of the aircraft may be necessary for maintenance reasons and the process is manually controlled via the FQMS, using the external refuel panel. Discharged fuel is collected via the refuel couplings.

In normal operations, refuelling is performed under full control of the FQMS. This automatic refuel can be initiated from the external refuel panel or from the cockpit. The FQMS can control the fuel loading and distribution to obtain a post-refuel CG of 39.5%. This is referred to as CG targeting. The crew can further refine the fuel distribution using Automatic Ground Transfer to obtain their desired target within ±1%.

Landing gear

With a maximum take-off weight (MTOW) of 575 tonnes and a typical maximum landing weight (MLW) of some 394 tonnes, the A380 required a substantial set of landing gear, capable of distributing the weight footprint of the aircraft. It was also important for the landing gear to be designed in such a way that it would allow the A380 to manoeuvre effectively on runways and taxiways at ICAO Code E and FAA Group V airports, more of which is explained in Chapter 7.

During the design and development phase, more than 38 landing gear configurations were considered. The final approved design consists of a 22-wheel array made up of two wing landing

RIGHT **Brand new landing gear components await installation on the final assembly line in Toulouse.** (Author)

gears (WLG) with four-wheel bogie assembly, two body landing gears (BLG) with six-wheel bogie assembly and the nose landing gear (NLG) with twin wheel assembly. The bogie assembly is the chassis or framework that carries the wheels, serving as a modular sub-assembly.

The WLGs are located under the wing and retract sideways towards the fuselage centreline, while the BLGs are located on the belly and retract rearward into a bay in the fuselage. The NLG retracts forward into a fuselage compartment below the cockpit.

A two-piece side-stay assembly holds each WLG in the extended position. A lock-stay keeps the side-stay assembly stable in the locked down position. Each BLG has a two-piece drag-stay assembly that mechanically locks the leg in the extended position.

The landing gear and operation of the landing gear doors are controlled electrically and are hydraulically and mechanically operated. In an abnormal operation, the landing gear can be extended using gravity.

RIGHT **The scale of the body landing gear (BLG) is immediately apparent on the British Airways A380.** (Author)

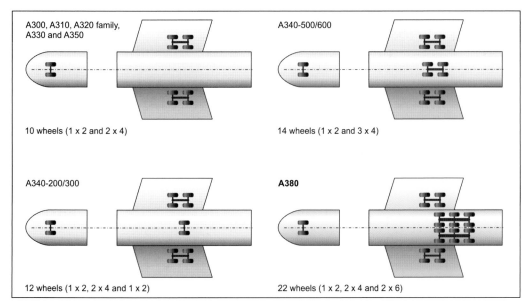

A300, A310, A320 family, A330 and A350

10 wheels (1 x 2 and 2 x 4)

A340-500/600

14 wheels (1 x 2 and 3 x 4)

A340-200/300

12 wheels (1 x 2, 2 x 4 and 1 x 2)

A380

22 wheels (1 x 2, 2 x 4 and 2 x 6)

LEFT **A comparison of landing gear configurations on the A380 and other aircraft in the Airbus family.** (Roy Scorer)

Steering control is mainly effected by the NLG wheel pair (nosewheel steering) and is further supported by the aft axle of the BLG which is also steerable to ensure better manoeuvrability for small-radius turns. A steering disconnection box is installed on the NLG to allow steering deactivation when the aircraft is towed.

To stop the A380, a combination of thrust reversers, together with enormous carbon composite Honeywell anti-skid brakes on 16 of the 20 main landing gear wheels (on each wheel of the WLG and on the wheels of the front and centre axles of the BLG) do most of the work. The braking system is electrically controlled and hydraulically operated. It works like the anti-skid brakes in your car, responding to extreme pressure by automatically pulsing to prevent brake lockup and skidding. Almost as important is the aerodynamic braking of 16 giant wing-top spoilers, which create drag and reduce lift. Reducing lift improves mechanical braking by putting more weight on the wheels.

Braking occurs automatically during the retraction of the landing gear. This stops the rotation of the BLG and WLG wheels before the landing gears go into their related bays.

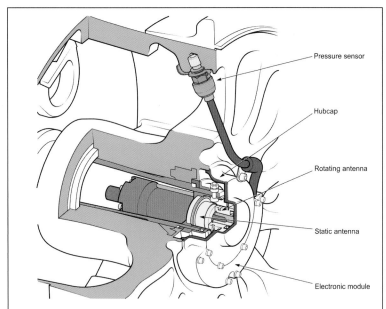

Pressure sensor

Hubcap

Rotating antenna

Static antenna

Electronic module

ABOVE The A380's tyre pressure monitoring system will trigger a warning if a tyre pressure is detected below a given percentage of the nominal tyre pressure. A warning will trigger if a differential pressure above a given percentage is detected across tyres on the same axle. *(Roy Scorer)*

RIGHT The aircraft's nosewheel can turn 70 degrees and the aft axle of the body landing gear is also steerable, enabling the giant A380 to manoeuvre around the world's airports. *(Roy Scorer)*

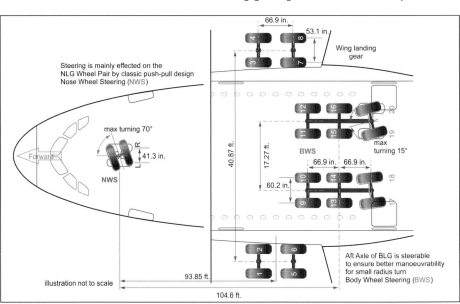

Steering is mainly effected on the NLG Wheel Pair by classic push-pull design Nose Wheel Steering (NWS)

max turning 70°

41.3 in.

NWS

Forward

illustration not to scale

93.85 ft.

104.6 ft.

66.9 in.

53.1 in.

Wing landing gear

40.87 ft.

17.27 ft.

60.2 in.

BWS

66.9 in.   66.9 in.

max turning 15°

Aft Axle of BLG is steerable to ensure better manoeuvrability for small radius turn
Body Wheel Steering (BWS)

Brake to Vacate

An innovative feature from Airbus was first introduced on the A380 and makes a real difference at airports with heavy traffic levels. As airports constantly strive to increase capacity by reducing the time aircraft spend on the runway after their landing touchdown, the aircraft's Brake to Vacate (BTV) system delivers significant improvements in runway efficiency.

The BTV system optimises braking efficiency and runway turnround time, with the potential of reducing runway occupancy time by up to 30%. Its improvements in landing traffic flow is so dramatic that airports are seeing a capacity increase of approximately 15% – while also providing additional benefits in terms of operational costs, improved safety and passenger comfort.

BTV allows pilots to select the appropriate runway exit during the approach to landing, and regulates the aircraft's deceleration after touchdown – enabling it to reach any chosen exit at the correct speed under optimum conditions, regardless of the weather and visibility.

Systems integration and redundancy

So advanced and integrated are the systems on the A380 that aviation commentators have viewed it as a step-change 'somewhere between the A320 and the Concorde' in the number of changes it introduces. The aircraft's size alone makes it a step-change because, in

ABOVE The A380's 22-wheel array is designed to support a maximum take-off weight of 569 tonnes. *(Waldo van der Waal)*

aircraft, complexity increases with size, as does the need for electrical, hydraulic and pneumatic systems capability.

As an example, the network server system/onboard information system (NSS/OIS) on the A380 provides a greater degree of integration between flight-control functions, sensors, avionics and systems control. This is all designed to provide the flight crew with full situational awareness and total aircraft control. The NSS could be likened to a central nervous system for the aircraft.

BELOW The A380 features unprecedented systems redundancy and was the first civil airliner capable of flying with a complete hydraulic failure. *(Lufthansa)*

The OIS is a fully integrated electronic flight bag (EFB) in its own right, containing an aircraft library with charts, aircraft and company manuals and a fully updatable aviation information services (AIS) database. The aircraft's size increases its unit price and consequently dispatch reliability becomes more critical so the aircraft also had to be designed with unprecedented systems redundancy and damage tolerance. For example, the A380 was designed to be the first civil air transport aircraft capable of flying with a total hydraulic failure, using electricity to operate only the flight control surfaces. It can also operate with only one electrical generation source, or only one hydraulic source.

Environmental considerations

Meeting the increasingly important environmental standards for air transportation today and in the future were among the key elements for the A380, which was designed in close collaboration with major airlines, airports and airworthiness authorities.

There is no doubt the aircraft makes a positive contribution to the ongoing environmental challenges faced by the aviation industry as air traffic growth reaches record numbers. Use of state-of-the-art engines which generate the lowest fuel consumption per seat contribute significantly to lower emission levels and better local air quality. For example, 105kg of fuel will be saved per passenger on a Paris–Tokyo round-trip flight – reinforcing the aircraft's position as an industry leader for eco-efficiency.

To best meet the needs of its customers and allow unrestricted operations worldwide, Airbus also implemented noise reduction design elements that include enhanced engine acoustic treatment and the optimisation of wing design. Noise levels on departure are half those of its nearest competitor and three to four times less when landing, while at the same time carrying 40% more passengers.

BELOW The A380 is an industry leader for eco-efficiency, with noise reduction design elements that include enhanced engine acoustic treatment and an optimal wing design. *(Airbus)*

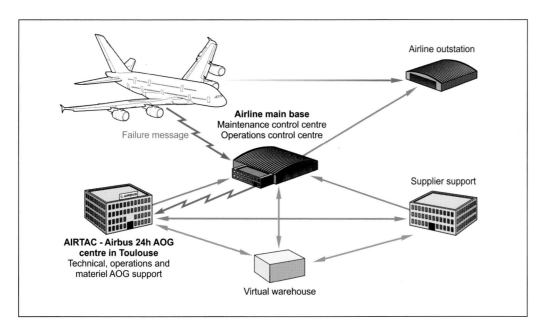

More passengers per flight enables airlines (and airports) to grow without adding additional flights – two essential factors given the high levels of congestion faced at airports around the world.

AIRTAC customer support

Airbus offers its customer airlines a unique support facility entitled AIRTAC (Airbus Technical Aircraft-on-ground Centre), based in Toulouse. The facility uses innovative, high-tech solutions to keep Airbus fleets around the world flying safely and efficiently. Specialist engineers based at the site are available around the clock to serve Airbus operators, working to minimise on-the-ground time for aircraft troubleshooting and repairs using state-of-the-art computer software and intuitive problem-solving skills.

An aircraft on the ground for any length of time is not generating income for an airline, so it is essential that any downtime is minimised to get the aircraft back into the skies once a repair has been safely executed, and given its size and passenger carrying ability, this is hugely relevant to the A380. There are further challenges too, as the size and weight of several components for the A380 are much greater than those for previous aircraft. For example, each air generation system unit in the wing root weighs 400kg, so the Airbus

design team had to make sure the removal and installation of replacement equipment was simple and safe for the engineering teams on the ground.

Fortunately help is at hand and the AIRTAC facility plays a vital role with the A380 fleet. Using its built-in test equipment and sophisticated communications platform, the A380 is able to relay messages automatically via the airline to AIRTAC in Toulouse about any technical problems it is experiencing during the flight. Before the airline calls the AIRTAC Centre, Airbus will have already prepared accurate procedures or recommendations to troubleshoot or undertake structural repairs. The centre also manages a database that provides information on the availability of spares for the A380 around the world, and can be interrogated automatically from the air. Once the problem has been identified and spare parts delivered to the aircraft, Airbus has also ensured the repair is achieved as quickly as possible.

To guard against a potential technical problem significantly delaying an A380 flight, Airbus set requirements for the time to remove and reinstall certain components to ensure parts can be replaced within the 2–3-hour turnround time for the aircraft.

The services and technical engineering resources on offer are ramped up by Airbus when a new customer reaches the service-entry phase and are there to ensure a smooth transition into operation.

CHAPTER 3

Production

OPPOSITE A Thai Airways A380 on the final assembly line (FAL) in Toulouse – the FAL itself is an engineering masterstroke. *(Airbus)*

Introduction

The epic proportions of the A380 are one
of aviation's most remarkable engineering
and logistical achievements. Although Airbus
has been designing and building aircraft for
nearly 40 years, the scale and requirements of
the A380 project meant the manufacturer not
only had to put all its past experience to use,
but also had to take many of its processes,
resources, skills and facilities to a new level of
ingenuity, productivity and creativity.

The A380 is a truly pan-European project,
with the major structural sections of the aircraft
built in France, Germany, Spain and the
United Kingdom. Given the sheer size of
these sections, traditional transportation
methods proved impractical, and a highly
specialised and complex logistics operation
had to be implemented to get these parts to the
FAL in Toulouse.

Much like the aircraft, the FAL itself is
an engineering masterstroke. It is Europe's
largest industrial building where cutting-edge

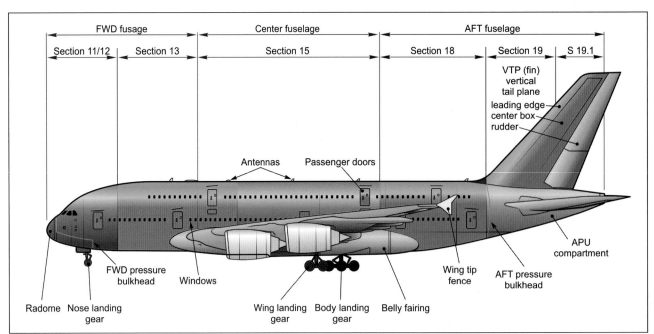

technology and materials – together with some of aviation's best engineers – bring together the sub-assemblies that create these wonderful flying machines.

This chapter will also look at the solutions Airbus found to some unexpected challenges once the aircraft had gone into production as well as the myriad tasks that need to be completed once the aircraft is built, including testing, cabin fit-out, painting and, finally, delivery and handover to the airline customer.

A collaborative project across Europe

Across Europe new assembly and sub-assembly facilities had to be set up using some of the most modern manufacturing tools and techniques in a highly synchronised operation capable of providing a network that would keep production of the super jumbo on track.

Different countries were assigned to produce the airliner's different components based on their areas of expertise:

■ **Germany** – Hamburg is the headquarters of Airbus in Germany and employs around 15,000 people, playing a key role in the development and engineering of all Airbus aircraft. The Hamburg site has overall responsibility for four important work packages for the A380, namely: structural assembly and equipment installation of all forward and aft fuselage sections, complete interior furnishing of the passenger cabin and the cargo compartment, painting of all A380 aircraft as well as final acceptance and delivery to customers in Europe and the Middle East. All the electronic communications and cabin management systems needed by both crew and passengers are designed and produced at the Buxtehude site in Germany. They include the cabin intercommunication data system used to control cabin functions and the passenger service units for seating system controls. The vertical tailplanes for all Airbus aircraft are produced at the company's Stade facility. In Stade, the rear pressure bulkhead and the vertical fin are produced.

■ **France** – engine pylons for Airbus's full product line of aircraft are designed and manufactured at the Saint-Eloi site in central Toulouse. Toulouse's responsibilities include engineering (general design, systems and integration tests, definition of the structure and more), structure testing and a materials processes development centre, systems organisation, flight tests, the Beluga hangar and one of Airbus's three delivery centres. It also hosts FALs for the A320, A350 XWB and A330 – including the cabin furnishing and painting – as well as the A380's final assembly and preparation for flight.

◆ Saint-Eloi is responsible for delivering equipped and tested pylons to the FALs. Its primary activities include the design of pylon and propulsion systems, integration and manufacturing of pylon and nacelle components including hard metal transformation, pylon sub-assembly and pylon integration for all Airbus aircraft.

◆ The Saint-Nazaire plant specialises in structural assembly, equipping and testing of front and central fuselage sections for the entire Airbus family. It receives the forward and central fuselage for the A380. Saint-Nazaire is also in charge of equipping and testing these sections before delivering them to various FALs.

◆ Nantes specialises in the manufacturing and assembly of the centre wing boxes for all Airbus aircraft, and is a leader in the manufacture of CFRP structural parts. Nantes is also responsible for manufacturing the radomes for the entire Airbus family, the ailerons and air inlets for the A380.

■ **United Kingdom** – located in North Wales, Airbus's Broughton site assembles wings for the entire family of commercial aircraft, producing over 1,000 wings per year. Its activities include wing skin milling, stringer manufacture, wing equipping and wing box assembly.

◆ Filton is the other UK-based site for Airbus, with its engineering and research and technology groups responsible for wing design, landing gear and fuel systems design and testing and manufacturing of components.

■ **Spain** – located in central Spain, the Airbus facility at Getafe specialises in aeronautical component engineering, design, production and assembly and uses metallic material and advanced composite materials to manufacture fuselage for all Airbus aircraft and specialises in the final assembly and systems testing of the A380 horizontal tailplane, rear fuselage, tail cone of the A380's main landing gear doors. The Airbus's Illescas site, to the south of Getafe, is a leader in the manufacture of composite aeronautical components, and focuses on stabilisers, rudders and spars, sections of rear fuselage and landing gear components for the A380. Located in the south of Spain, Puerto Real specialises in automated assembly of movable surfaces (rudders and spars) for all Airbus programmes. It also is responsible for final equipment and delivery to the FAL of large, complex structural components – such as the horizontal tailplane and belly fairing of the A380 fuselage.

In support of manufacturing the main elements, more than 200 key suppliers were called upon to produce additional components. The majority of these are based in Europe, with others located in the USA and even Australia. At the peak of the project's development, 6,400 engineers were working full-time on the endeavour. The aircraft was described at the time as 'essentially a European product, representing not only a magnificent new page in the history of aviation, but a glorious new chapter for European aviation'.

Multimodal transportation system

Airbus knew it would be physically impossible to produce all the key components for the A380 in one location and that it would have to make use of multiple production sites across Europe. While this in itself was a pretty audacious objective, getting components with exceptional dimensions to the

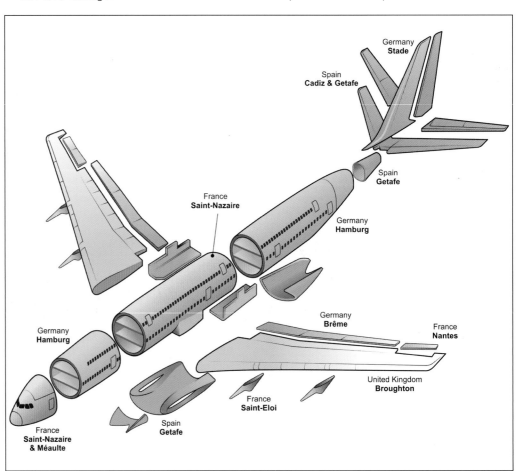

RIGHT Components for the A380 are produced across Europe. *(Roy Scorer)*

FAL in Toulouse would present a whole new set of challenges.

For most of the manufacturer's other logistics requirements, it has at its disposal a fleet of five Airbus A300-600ST Beluga aircraft that transport parts from sites across Europe to Toulouse for the assembly of everything from the Airbus A318 to the A350. Given the size of the A380 sections, Airbus could not make use of this system and had to devise a new transport system making use of a huge purpose-built ship, barges and road trailers. The only exception for the A380 is the vertical tailplane and rudder that can, in fact, be accommodated in the Beluga.

Airbus manufactures the A380's key components – the wings, the tailfins and fuselage sections – in facilities in the United Kingdom, Spain, Germany and France. Each is then shipped to Bordeaux in France. Together they are put on a barge to the French town of Langon and from there each segment is loaded on to the back of a truck, forming a remarkable convoy that is led by a large police escort across some 124 miles of countryside to the Airbus FAL.

The overall water and road route created to allow the transport of the outsize structural

ABOVE Airbus uses its own fleet of A300-600ST Beluga aircraft to transport the vertical tail plane to Toulouse. *(Airbus)*

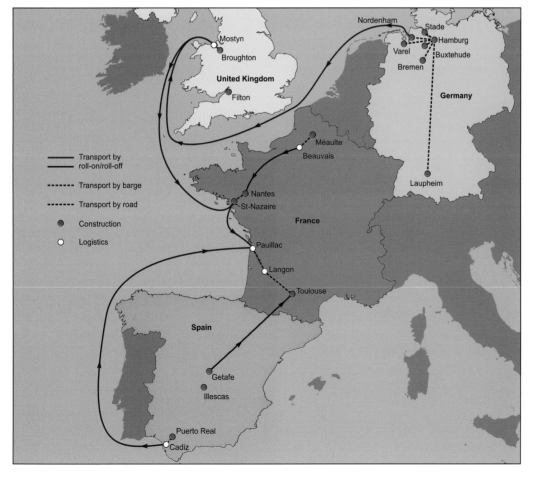

LEFT This map demonstrates the remarkable logistics operation established by Airbus to get key components to the final assembly line. *(Roy Scorer)*

sections to Toulouse is known as the IGG or Itinéraire à Grand Gabarit and involved the modification of existing waterways and public roads, as well as the addition of some new road sections. The road route itself was largely determined by the need to avoid bridges and many adjustments were necessary to road junctions to allow the convoys to pass. In some places, new roads were constructed, some of which are exclusively reserved for the use of the convoys. Convoys travel mostly at night, laying over during the day at specially constructed secure parking areas.

The Ro-Ro (roll-on/roll-off) ships in service measure 127m–155m in length, are 25m wide and have been specifically sized to transport A380 components. Each ship follows a particular route sailing to the ports serving the Airbus plants located in Broughton (United Kingdom), Hamburg (Germany), Puerto Real (Spain) and Saint-Nazaire (France).

At Broughton the 45m wings are assembled and, once tested, they are brought 17 miles up the River Dee aboard a barge to the Port of Mostyn before being transferred to the specially designed Ro-Ro vessel for transportation to Toulouse. The wings are covered in plastic to protect them from the elements – particularly

saltwater ingress – during the transfer to Toulouse. The ship then sails to Pauillac.

At the same time, the *City of Hamburg* leaves Hamburg port with the rear part of the fuselage and continues on to Saint-Nazaire to load the other parts of the centre and forward fuselage. Loaded with all the aircraft fuselage elements, the boat then sails to Pauillac to deliver its cargo.

Meanwhile, other vessels sail to the ports of Naples in Italy, Cádiz (Puerto Real) in Spain and Saint-Nazaire, before continuing to Pauillac, loaded with the horizontal tailplane and the sub-assemblies of the fuselage and the aircraft floor.

The part of the nose section of the fuselage which contains the cockpit is sub-assembled at another French site, Méaulte, and sent by road to Saint-Nazaire.

The aircraft components are then transferred to a floating pontoon located on the Gironde Estuary near Pauillac. There, two 75m-long barges transport the components 56 miles up the Garonne to Langon, passing through the centre of Bordeaux. The barges incorporate ballast tanks to enable them to adjust their water and air draughts to the prevailing conditions. For example, certain parts of the route must be undertaken at high tide in order to provide

BELOW The rear fuselage section is loaded at the port of Hamburg. *(Airbus)*

ABOVE LEFT An A380 wing is loaded onto a barge for its journey up the River Dee. *(Airbus)*

ABOVE The wing is transferred from the barge to a special roll-on/roll-off vessel. *(Airbus)*

LEFT Loaded on a barge, the centre fuselage section passes under the Pont de Pierre in the centre of Bordeaux – crews ensure they pass through on a low tide. *(Airbus)*

sufficient water under the keel, while the passage under the Pont de Pierre in Bordeaux is undertaken at low tide to provide sufficient clearance for the components under the bridge.

A specially constructed dock has been built in Langon to facilitate the offloading of parts. Four return journeys (over eight days) between Pauillac and Langon are required to ship all the components.

The Canal de Garonne allows barges to reach Toulouse but has insufficient headroom for the A380's parts. This means the final leg of this monumental logistics exercise is done by road, when the six components delivered to Langon depart on a convoy of trucks – six sets of specially designed trailers with their tractors – and move in two stages, from Eauze to L'Isle Jourdain, and then on to the FAL in Toulouse.

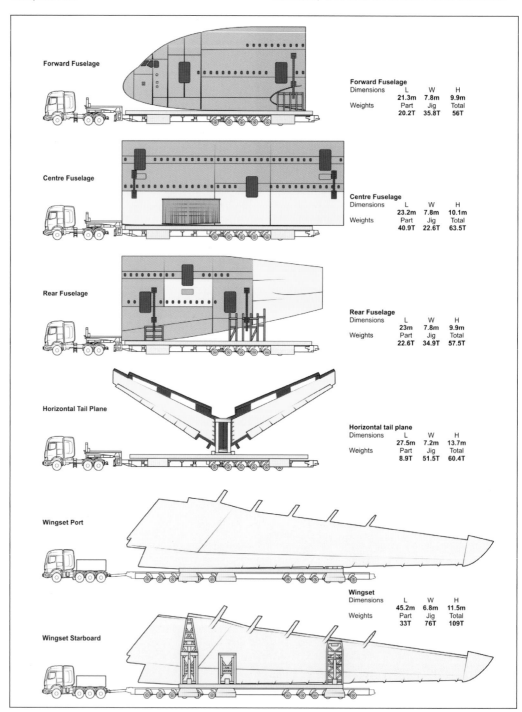

Forward Fuselage

Forward Fuselage			
Dimensions	L	W	H
	21.3m	7.8m	9.9m
Weights	Part	Jig	Total
	20.2T	35.8T	56T

Centre Fuselage

Centre Fuselage			
Dimensions	L	W	H
	23.2m	7.8m	10.1m
Weights	Part	Jig	Total
	40.9T	22.6T	63.5T

Rear Fuselage

Rear Fuselage			
Dimensions	L	W	H
	23m	7.8m	9.9m
Weights	Part	Jig	Total
	22.6T	34.9T	57.5T

Horizontal Tail Plane

Horizontal tail plane			
Dimensions	L	W	H
	27.5m	7.2m	13.7m
Weights	Part	Jig	Total
	8.9T	51.5T	60.4T

Wingset Port

Wingset Starboard

Wingset			
Dimensions	L	W	H
	45.2m	6.8m	11.5m
Weights	Part	Jig	Total
	33T	76T	109T

RIGHT The six major sections that form part of the overnight convoy from Langdon to Toulouse.
(Roy Scorer)

FAR LEFT Massive jigs on specially designed trailers are used to support the wings during their final leg of the journey. *(Author)*

LEFT Given their cylindrical shape, the fuselage sections are held in place by special clamps. *(Author)*

BELOW The A380 wings – transferred by both barge and ferry – are wrapped in plastic for protection from the elements. *(Author)*

JOINING THE CONVOY

The opportunity to see the A380 convoy first-hand was a once-in-a-lifetime experience. Arriving at the floodlit rest area well after dark, one is instantly blown away by the size and scale of the parts. And it's not only the aircraft parts that impress – the mighty jigs that secure these to the trailers are remarkable sculptures in their own right.

The wings are gigantic, each on its own trailer, wrapped tightly in plastic. They sit at the front of the convoy like huge arrows, pointing the way forward for the rest of the fleet. One can only marvel at the massive tailfin, itself as big as the wings on an Airbus A320. It looks finely balanced on its weighty jig and one can't help but smile and think of this as the biggest model set you've ever seen. Beneath the tailfin are stacked crates labelled with part names like 'Right Inboard Elevator' and 'Left Trailing Edge', and there is an urge to open the crates and put the 'kit' together yourself, right there and then.

And then there are the three huge fuselage sections, each with protective covers bearing

RIGHT The aircraft's horizontal tail plane stands almost 14m high and includes an integral fuel tank. *(Author)*

LEFT Additional components are packaged up and transported with the convoy. *(Author)*

ABOVE The convoy prepares to depart one of the specially constructed roadside stops used exclusively by Airbus as somewhere for the vehicles to wait during the day. *(Author)*

BELOW The centre wing box is clearly visible on the central fuselage section. *(Author)*

BELOW RIGHT The rear fuselage section that will ultimately hold the vertical tail fin and horizontal stabiliser. *(Author)*

LEFT Additional components are packaged up and transported with the convoy. *(Author)*

the Airbus logo. Each piece dominates your field of vision under the lights and it is hard to believe that at some point in the near future you might well be sitting in the cabin of this very aircraft.

Time at the rest stop is limited and it is instantly apparent just how precise and refined the convoy programme has become – it's a fine art and expertly executed. The countdown to departure commences and each of the bright yellow support vehicles starts to take its position; flashing lights adorn the area. An advance party on two wheels heads off first, making sure that the road ahead is clear. There can be no hold-ups once this mammoth procession starts moving. The convoy travels 149 miles at a speed of 6–15mph and the complete road train can be up to 1.2 miles in length, including the accompanying vehicles, transport service, police and security.

The route passes through several small French villages and we race ahead to Gimont where the convoy passes over a bridge and then takes a sharp left-hand turn into the village. Fortunately the road through this small town is of a reasonable size but in some of the smaller hamlets, like Levignac, the convoy literally passes within inches of some of the buildings. Locals are looking out of their windows, some are out on the streets and there is an air of anticipation from the first sets of flashing lights;

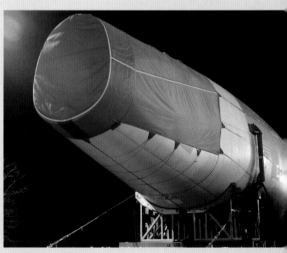

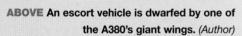

ABOVE An escort vehicle is dwarfed by one of the A380's giant wings. *(Author)*

ABOVE RIGHT The supporting jig for an A380 wing weighs more than double the weight of the wing itself. *(Author)*

soon the convoy is there and the gigantic parts wind their way through town. 'C'est spectaculaire!'

By now it's well past midnight and immediately behind the convoy follows a team that replaces any road signs removed to make way for the trailers and does a sweep of the route to ensure all is in order for when the roads are reopened to the public.

The following morning, on a site visit to the FAL, we are reunited with the set of parts we saw just a few hours ago. They are perfectly lined up outside the huge Airbus assembly hangar and in the bright morning sunshine they look even more impressive than they did under lights. As the assembly teams arrive for work at the plant I want to help open the boxes and make the model. After all, I was part of the convoy that got it there!

ABOVE The A380's wings are the largest ever built for a commercial airliner. *(Author)*

BELOW Safely in Toulouse, the three fuselage sections sit in the early morning sunshine before being moved into the assembly hall. *(Author)*

Wings

Arguably the greatest technical innovation and most revolutionary aspect of the A380 is its highly complex and enormously efficient wing design, capable of lifting 560 tonnes to an altitude of 12,000m.

The wings are one of the most critical structural components in the entire aircraft and play host to a variety of technical systems, including some 23 miles of wiring, piping and ducting to drive the aircraft's flight control surfaces. As well as providing lift, the wings also house the aircraft's fuel tanks and pumps. Most of the fuel that can take the A380 to its maximum range of 15,000km is stored in the wings, so this means some 120,000 litres of flammable fluid, weighing 115 metric tonnes is contained in each wing. To add to the already significant load, the wings also carry the aircraft's four engines, each weighing around 6.5 tonnes.

Opened in July 2003, the Airbus wing manufacturing plant in Broughton, North Wales, is the largest manufacturing site in the UK, producing wings for the A320, A330/A340, A350 and A380 aircraft.

The site's dedicated A380 facility, known as the 'West Factory', is more than 400m long and 200m wide, resulting in a floor area equivalent to that of 12 full-size football pitches. More than 10,000 tonnes of steelwork was used to build the factory and the concrete piles run more than 30m deep into the ground – meaning the building is almost as deep as it is high.

Some 6,000 employees work at the facility, nestled among farmland close to the Wales–England border. The area has long been associated with the aviation industry, dating back to when a large aircraft factory was completed in 1939 for use by British engineering conglomerate, Vickers-Armstrongs, who built 5,786 Wellington bombers at the site. More than 2,800 De Havilland aircraft were built at the facility in the post-war period.

Its ultra-modern facilities today house the main assembly jigs, where the wing components and sub-assemblies are loaded and assembled, and a wing-equipping area where fuel, pneumatic and hydraulic systems and wiring are installed. A set of wings comprises more than 32,000 individual parts.

The wing-manufacturing process itself consists of creating a core wing structure made of a framework of spars and ribs. The three rear spars are set in place first and these run the full length of the wing to create its spine. Further spars are added in the centre and at the front of the framework, with 49 aluminium and carbon fibre composite ribs then crossing the spars and extending from the leading to the trailing edges of the wing. The design and arrangement of this internal structure ensures the wing is not only light and strong to cope with the enormous

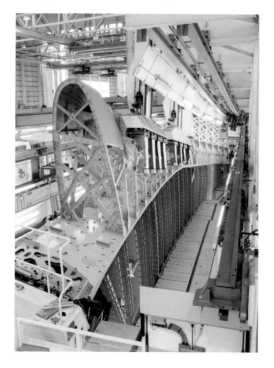

loads it is subjected to, but it also enables the wings to bend in exactly the right way. The A380's wings will, on take-off, twist as well as rise at their tips by a full 4m.

The framework of spars and ribs are used to support the aluminium panels that make up the outside skin of the wing.

The panels – each of which has a specific shape and weight requirement – are then further reinforced by a series of aluminium stringers. Attaching the panels to both the stringers and the underlying spar-and-rib framework requires positioning, drilling and then riveting or bolting about 180,000 holes.

The panels themselves are produced from raw material in a separate operation and this process begins with what is called skin-milling, where single pieces of aluminium alloy up to 35m in length are milled to the panel shape defined by the 3D contour map stored in the machine's computer. The process is painstaking and can take up to three days, despite these being the largest machines of their kind in Europe.

With weight a paramount consideration, all unnecessary scraps of metal are milled away and ultimately there is more aluminium left in waste than there is remaining on the panel – though of course this all gets recycled. The panels pass through a surface treatment plant

and are subjected to 12 different treatment baths to clean, degrease, anodise and protect them prior to assembly.

The panels are creep-formed to lock in the desired aerodynamic curve using moulds and heat-treating them – in one of the largest pressurised heat chambers in Europe – over a 24-hour period at a uniform 150°C across the oven. Precise temperature control is essential and anything outside of agreed tolerances will invalidate the process, rendering the wing useless.

ABOVE Each wing panel has a specific weight and shape and is produced by a process called skin-milling. *(Author)*

LEFT After the wing structure has been assembled it is moved to the station where equipment and systems are fitted, including fuel systems, pumps, hydraulics and the electrical harnesses. *(Airbus)*

RIGHT A partially completed wing being moved between stations. *(Airbus)*

The actual wing production process is based around six key stages, as follows:

- **Stage 00** – low-voltage electro-magnetic riveting machines (LVERs) are used to automatically drill, rivet and bolt stringers to the wing panels, helping to speed up the riveting process.
- **Stage 01** – the main assembly jigs act as a construction frame and hold the wings as they are being assembled – they are the biggest jigs used in aviation history. The areas in front of the jigs (known as the 'washing lines') are where the panels wait to be loaded into the jig; they are positioned, drilled, countersunk, riveted or bolted with titanium locking bolts on to the pre-drilled framework. Innovative automatic computer-controlled drilling techniques are used on the main jigs. These include portable horizontal automatic wing drilling equipment (HAWDE) which can be used at different levels of the jigs and gear rib automated wing drilling equipment (GRAWDE) which drills the heavily strengthened and reinforced area where the landing gear is later attached.
- **Stage 02** – with the structure now intact, an entire wing is raised up clear of the main assembly jigs by the overhead cranes. The wing is lifted from hoist points close to where the engines are ultimately located as these are the strongest parts of the wing. It needs to pass through a narrow gap as it is raised off the jig and at 400m^2 in size, this is a very delicate process – any damage to the wing will cause major production delays and substantial disruption to the Europe-wide logistics operation. The wings are then turned horizontally, checked and then carried through the building on a low raft before being moved into the equipping area.
- **Stage 03** – this is the equipping stage and sees the fitting of hydraulics, pneumatic systems, fuel systems and wiring. As the wing is integral to braking and steering, it is home to more than 23 miles of wiring and three complex hydraulic systems.
- **Stage 04** – the penultimate stage sees the wing head to the high-tech paint shop and it is then wrapped (to protect it from the elements) and prepared for shipment.
- **Stage 05** – the final stage caters for the dispatch of the wings and a multi-purpose vehicle (MPV) is used to transport each wing on a 1-mile journey to the River Dee. The MPV moves along a specially constructed track, its 96 wheels following a wire guidance

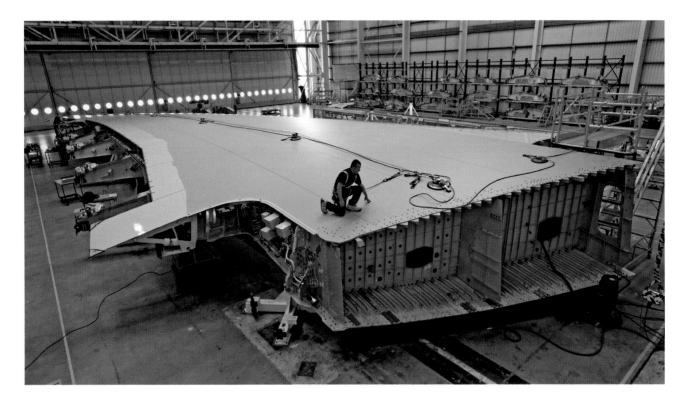

system. The vehicle is 22m long and with the wing and supporting jig together, carries around 140 tonnes. The MPV drives on board the River Dee craft to place the wing in position and one wing is transported at a time on the 17-mile river journey to the Port of Mostyn. Here a complete set is transferred by another MPV and put on to a vessel for onward transportation to the FAL in Toulouse.

Such is the attention to detail that all of the components used, including the smallest bolts and rivets, are accompanied by paperwork detailing the origin, supplier, batch of base metal, date and time of manufacture origins so that there is accountability in the event of a malfunction.

Wing facts
- Each set of wings has 30 panels and 314 stringers, 750,000 rivets or bolts and 23 miles of wiring
- Each wing is 45m long (with curve), 11m wide and 3m deep
- Behind the scenes, a logistics department co-ordinates orders from more than 100 different global partners and suppliers on every continent – except Antarctica
- A finished wing will weigh around 30 tonnes.

FATIGUE TESTING

Like any new commercial airliner going into service, the A380 underwent significant fatigue testing as part of its certification programme. Much of the testing was conducted at a purpose-built test laboratory in Dresden, Germany, where a 1,800-tonne test rig was constructed. A full-scale A380 airframe was then constructed in a purpose-built hangar and testing lasted for some 26 months.

During testing, computer modelling of actual flight scenarios was used in conjunction with a network of 180 hydraulic rams designed to stress test by bending and distorting the wings to expose any weaknesses in their structure. Pneumatic loading facilities were also used to pressurise the cabin.

Airbus artificially recreated 60,800 flight cycles, corresponding to more than three times the 25 years of service life for an A380. This helped the manufacturer to better understand how the aircraft would respond to various stresses over a long period of time and during different stages of its operations, such as taxiing on the runway, take-off, cruising and landing.

During these tests, the aircraft was pushed to its limits, simulating around 900 test flights a week, meaning the stresses incurred during a 16-hour flight could be simulated in just 11 minutes.

WING-RIB HAIRLINE CRACKS

When Airbus commenced with repairs to the Qantas A380 that suffered an engine disintegration near Singapore in November 2010, a fundamental part of the process was to check the assumption that the damage revealed in the post-incident inspections was in fact caused by that incident.

The rigours of the investigation revealed two issues, neither of which could be linked to the stresses imposed by the disintegrating engine. The first were tiny cracks found on the feet of the wing brackets used to join the wing's skin to the ribs, those elements that form the wing's internal structure. Each A380 wing contains around 2,000 L-shaped brackets of this kind.

The second series of cracks – discovered in two aircraft during a routine two-year inspection – were found in the vertical flange of the wing rib. Airbus publicly acknowledged the issue, emphasising that the cracks did not affect the safe operation of the aircraft. The European Aviation Safety Authority (EASA) issued a bulletin mandating precautionary checks. The EASA required Airbus to inspect all of the 20 A380s that had accumulated significant cycles to gain a clear picture on which to base any further longer-term measures.

For Airbus, it was vital to determine whether what was happening to the brackets was occurring on the factory floor, during the transfer from the UK to the FAL in Toulouse, or for some other, as yet undiscovered reason. Whatever the cause, it needed to be established – and eliminated.

Airbus ultimately concluded that during the manufacturing process, unintended additional stress had caused a very small number of these brackets to develop hairline cracks. As they had no safety of flight implications, these brackets were replaced during the next major scheduled airframe maintenance routine. It took Airbus around nine months to find and certify a solution for both existing and new aircraft. High-strength aluminium reinforced with carbon fibre had initially been used to reduce weight, but new sets of the more critical brackets were subsequently made from standard aluminium, increasing weight by 90kg. Costs of the remedial work are estimated to have been around £435m, excluding the additional cost of compensation paid to the airlines for taking aircraft out of service (for two months each) to inspect and carry out the work.

To their credit, Airbus adopted a proactive stance and dealt with the matter early to reassure both current and prospective airline customers as well as the flying public.

In the words of A380 Chief Engineer, John Roberts:

One of the lessons of more than 40 years of airliner engineering is that when you see something you don't expect to find at a particular time in an airframe, you have to find out what it might lead to in a mature airframe. The right time to do this is in a young aircraft, not an aged one.

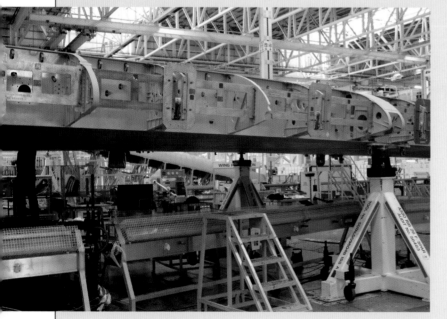

BELOW Airbus dealt quickly and proactively once the wing rib cracking issue had been discovered. *(Author)*

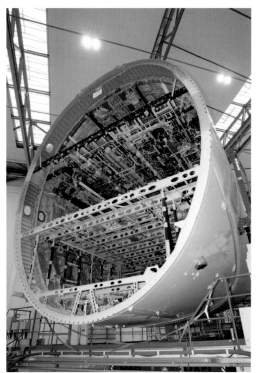

FAR LEFT An A380 fuselage section being assembled. The three levels of the aircraft – cargo, main deck and upper deck, can be easily distinguished. *(Airbus)*

LEFT The rear section of fuselage nearing the end of assembly. *(Airbus)*

Fuselage

The A380's fuselage shell segments are highly durable structures, welded together via laser instead of using conventional rivets.

Laser beam welding has become an integral part of the production chain for aircraft structures and metallic system components. By using this technique, new construction methods have been implemented that were not previously possible. The technology is ten times faster than the comparable riveting process and helps to achieve significant weight savings.

Production of the fuselage sections sees use made of Glare™ material in the pressurised fuselage's upper and lateral shells. This composite construction – a sandwich material made from alternating layers of aluminium

LEFT The tail section and rear fuselage are connected and ready for transportation to the final assembly line. *(Airbus)*

(0.3mm–0.5mm) and fibreglass with a reinforced adhesive (bond film) – has its properties optimised by adjusting the number of plies and orientation of the glass tapes.

Fibreglass tends to have low impact strength but strong load resistance, while aluminium has low load resistance and high impact resistance. The end product is a superior material which offers a significant reduction in weight (of some 30% when compared with conventional aluminium alloys) and provides advanced fatigue and damage resistance characteristics.

Outstanding fatigue resistance and impact properties, impressive mechanical properties, solid fire resistance and lightning strike resistance are some of Glare's™ many desirable attributes.

COMPOSITE WING BOX

A wing box is the structural component from which the wings extend. It is located at the junction between the wings and the fuselage and, when it was first designed, the A380's was a world's first, with more than 40% of the structure being made from carbon fibre with a total weight of 11 tonnes. This trend has continued with increasing levels of composite material now being used in new Airbus aircraft like the A350.

The A380's composite wing box – made in Nantes – is more resistant to wear and corrosion and lighter than metal. The weight gain of 1.5 tonnes (aided by fasteners made of titanium) generates a sizeable reduction in fuel-burn.

Airbus centre wing box characteristics

	Weight	Composite percentage	Length	Width	Weight gain with composites	Number of fasteners
A320	1.4t	0	3m	4.4m	0	15,000
A330	8.25t	0	6.9m	6.2m	0	35,000
A350	5.2t	50%	5.5m	6.5m	–1t	15,000
A380	11.3t	40%	6.9m	7.88m	–1.5t	15,000

Final assembly line

The total assembly process for an A380 lasts about eight months, half of which is carried out in Toulouse (assembly and testing) and half in Hamburg (cabin fitting and painting).

The industrial process of assembling the A380 on the FAL is organised along a north–south axis. The various sub-assemblies that make up the convoy arrive by road at the northern end of the Jean-Luc Lagardère site in the early hours. The sub-assemblies are unloaded using self-propelled vehicles before being taken to the FAL.

General assembly is carried out at a single combined workstation – known as 'Station 40'. Here, all the major assembly operations are performed – with the exception of engine installation – on a giant jig (think of it as the most elaborate scaffold structure you have ever seen) which allows the plane to come together.

The jig is comprised of two major components – one structure around the front of the aircraft which runs from the front of the wings, and another to access the wings and rear section. The front section of the jig is fixed in place and anchored to the ground, providing the stability and accuracy needed during the assembly process. The rear section of the jig moves on a set of tracks, allowing it to shift

FINKENWERDER – AIRBUS PLANT IN HAMBURG

Hamburg Finkenwerder is the headquarters of Airbus in Germany, employing around 12,500 people and playing a key role in the development and manufacturing of all Airbus aircraft.

From an A380 perspective, the plant is home to the aircraft's major component assembly hall, which houses the structural assembly and the equipping of the forward and complete rear fuselage sections. These fully assembled and equipped fuselage sections are produced here and then shipped to the A380 FAL in Toulouse.

In the production domain, Hamburg's many years of manufacturing experience in fuselage structural assembly and systems installation make this site a centre of competence for fuselage and cabin structures. In the engineering domain, key competences in Hamburg revolve mainly around the development of fuselage structure and the design, innovation and systems of the cabin. Following final assembly in Toulouse, A380s are fitted with their cabin interiors and painted for final delivery in Hamburg. Final acceptance and delivery of A380s for customers in Europe and the Middle East also takes place from Hamburg.

Close to the commercial airport of Hamburg-Fuhlsbüttel, Airbus operates a large spares centre – the facility holds some 120,000 proprietary parts, as well as a 24/7 spares call centre for its customers around the world.

Hamburg also plays a vital role in Airbus's hugely successful A320 family of aircraft; around half of the company's annual production of A320s are assembled, painted and delivered to customers from the Hamburg site.

LEFT The vertical tail plane of an A380 belonging to Qatar Airways is positioned prior to attaching it to the rear fuselage section. *(Airbus)*

LEFT The time an aircraft spends at Station 40 is driven by the current rate of production – the plant is capable of producing up to four super jumbos a month. *(Airbus)*

out of the way when the aircraft moves to the next station.

The jig enables the three fuselage sections to be mated, the wings, horizontal and vertical stabilisers to be attached, the engine pylons, landing gear and wheels mounted and the electronic racks installed. The pre-stressed wings are adjusted with the help of lasers and fitted to the wing box with around 4,000 magnesium, steel and titanium bolts and rivets.

The time an A380 spends in the jig at Station 40 is largely dependent on production requirements at that point in time. The plant's capacity allows it to turn out four A380s a month, which would see an aircraft in the jig for a little more than a week. And there is no respite for the assembly teams – on either side, adjacent to the jig, are the next set of wings being prepared with components, and in front

LEFT The forward fuselage section is the last major component to enter Station 40. *(Airbus)*

BELOW LEFT Station 40 is used to join the massive parts of the fuselage and wings together. *(Author)*

BELOW A laser-aided spatial positioning system is used to align the jigs and sub-assemblies with astonishing precision. *(Airbus)*

LEFT A completed wing is moved into position by overhead crane for mating with the fuselage. *(Airbus)*

of those are a set still wrapped in their white protective covering, fresh from the convoy that arrived that very morning.

With assembly of the major components complete, the aircraft is released from the jig, backed out of the building and taken through the next giant door to one of three slots known as Station 30. Here the interior systems are added – electrical, hydraulics, landing gear, the cockpit, doors and engine installations.

The work teams are a hugely skilled and versatile outfit. Tasks include raising the fuselage high enough to allow the landing gear to be installed from below; only then can the giant A380 finally be lowered down to rest on its own weight. The installation of the cables that run from the flight deck to the actuators – the electric motors that control the wing flaps and hinges – takes place here too. Instead of the outdated use of cables, the A380 uses electrical impulses in all of its control systems. This 'fly-by-wire' technology saves weight and is considered more reliable.

An aircraft is based at Station 30 for around three weeks, following which it is taken outside for a month-long series of final checks that include cabin pressurisation, landing gear,

CENTRE A Thai Airways A380 nears completion at Station 40 in Toulouse. *(Airbus)*

RIGHT Cockpit fit-out is a complex part of the production process and is handled by a specialist team. *(Martyn Cartledge)*

RIGHT The complete landing gear system can be retracted after take-off in just 20 seconds, including the closing of the large landing gear doors. *(Author)*

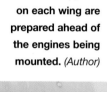

BELOW Two pylons on each wing are prepared ahead of the engines being mounted. *(Author)*

moving parts, hydraulic systems, radar, navigation, fuel leaks and engine tests.

Once mounted, the engines are then tested in the engine run-up area. Generally speaking, engines are the property of the aircraft's owners even before they take delivery of their aircraft. The airlines themselves negotiate the purchase of the engines directly from Rolls-Royce or Engine Alliance, and Airbus does not get involved in this process.

There is an overwhelming sense of calm and quiet across the FAL. Part of this is a result of the production line not running at full capacity (it was initially designed to deal with around 50 aircraft a year and it's currently completing fewer than 20), but the industrial racket that one might normally associate with a production line simply isn't there. Small teams beaver away doing what seem to be very delicate tasks on the mammoth beasts at Station 30.

Final preparation for flight takes around ten days before the aircraft makes its first test flight, and then heads to Hamburg where the cabin is fitted out (this takes around six weeks) and the aircraft is painted in the customer airline's livery.

LEFT Engine 3 is attached to this Emirates A380, with engine 4 to follow – the two engines on each wing add an additional 12 tonnes in weight. *(Author)*

TOULOUSE – FRANCE'S AVIATION HUB

Toulouse has a long history of aviation that began back in 1917 when French engineer Pierre-Georges Latécoère – backed by the French government – established an aircraft manufacturing company in the city.

As the First World War was coming to an end, the company opened the first civilian international airmail service when mail was flown from Toulouse to Barcelona in Spain. By February 1919 the airmail service had been extended to Casablanca in Morocco, making Latécoère Airlines the first transcontinental airmail service. In the early years of aviation, air races were held at Toulouse attracting crowds of up to 200,000 spectators.

Arguably the most famous pilot flying for Latécoère was Antoine de Saint-Exupéry who wrote about his experiences in the books *Wind, Sand and Stars* and *Night Flight*. In 1927 Latécoère renamed his company l'Aéropostale; it was then sold and ultimately became part of Air France. After the Second World War, Toulouse's association with aviation continued with new research and development facilities

established in the area and its stature as a hub for the European aviation sector started to gain significant momentum. This enviable position was further boosted when Airbus established its headquarters in Toulouse in 1974. The location is also notable as this was where Concorde made its first flight in 1969.

Today Aerospace Valley is a cluster of French aerospace engineering companies and research centres located in the regions of Occitaine and Nouvelle Aquitaine in the south-west of France, mainly concentrated in and around the city of Toulouse.

The 500-plus affiliated companies (including Airbus, Air France Industries and Dassault Aviation) provide some 130,000 jobs in the aviation and space flight industries. The cluster has initiated more than 220 research projects. Key facilities include aviation schools, aerospace research laboratories and state-of-the-art training facilities.

With exciting new projects like the Airbus A350, Toulouse sits at the very centre of the European aeronautical industry.

ABOVE A fully assembled Malaysian Airlines A380 departs Toulouse on a test flight prior to being flown to Hamburg for painting and cabin furnishing. *(Airbus)*

Built between 2002 and 2004, the Jean-Luc Lagardère complex is located in Blagnac near Toulouse. The gigantic 10-hectare purpose-built plant in Toulouse illustrates the enormity of the challenge Airbus has undertaken to assemble the world's largest commercial airliner.

For an airport to have a major airline construction facility co-located with a growing international passenger and freight hub is both unusual and unique – the airport is the sixth largest in France in terms of passenger numbers.

The A380 production facility is named after former President of the Lagardère group, an EADS (former Airbus Group) shareholder and a decisive player in the launch of the A380 programme. Before his death in 2003, Lagardère had interests in Formula 1, Le Mans, magazine publishing and was also a prominent figure in French horse racing.

The dimensions of the central hangar are impressive: 490m long, 250m wide and 46m high and the facility provides for some 122,500m^2 of floor area. Foundations for the building run 100m deep – not only to deal with the weight of the aircraft but also to ensure perfect accuracy when the fuselage and wing sections are joined together and the engineering teams are dealing with tolerances of much less than a millimetre.

At two-and-a-half times the size of the plant where Airbus's A330s are assembled, the Jean-Luc Lagardère plant is entirely dedicated to the final assembly of the A380 and its preparation for flight. Erected in under two years, the plant contains 32,000 tonnes of steel, four times more than the Eiffel Tower and as much as the Millau Viaduct. The overall plant houses not only the largest industrial building in Europe, but also provides for some 20 hectares of outdoor tarmac, taxiways that provide access to the airport's runways, an energy and fluid production plant, a fuel station, offices, company restaurants, a congress centre and associated services.

The estimated investment by Airbus in the plant is around £370 million.

BELOW The A380's dedicated and absolutely gigantic final assembly line (FAL) in Toulouse – the largest industrial building in Europe. *(Airbus)*

A further 14 days are built into the production schedule for flight line test activities before inspection by and delivery to the airline.

There is a big difference in terms of production philosophy with what happens on the FAL in Toulouse compared to that in Seattle, home of Airbus's rival, Boeing. At the latter's Everett plant, much of the 747 structure is built in one place, so it is a more traditional production line, with the accompanying noise of riveting and drilling. It's very much where the aircraft get built, whereas the spread of component production for Airbus across Europe has led to them adopting rather different manufacturing and final assembly processes to that of Boeing.

Cabin furnishing

Well before an A380 reaches the cabin engineering, definition and fit-out stage in Hamburg, the airline will have visited Airbus in Toulouse to see full-scale mock-up interiors of the aircraft and develop concept ideas and individual preferences.

Installation of the approved cabin design and features takes around 30 days, depending on the complexity of an airline's requirements. Installing row after row of economy seats will undoubtedly be an easier task compared to the high-end first-class offerings that in Qatar Airways' case, for example, include a separate living space, bathroom and double bed.

Work is typically divided up into different installation zones spread across the upper,

ABOVE Thermal and acoustic insulation is installed to address the key needs of cold, heat, sound and fire insulation before the interior trim panels are added. *(Author)*

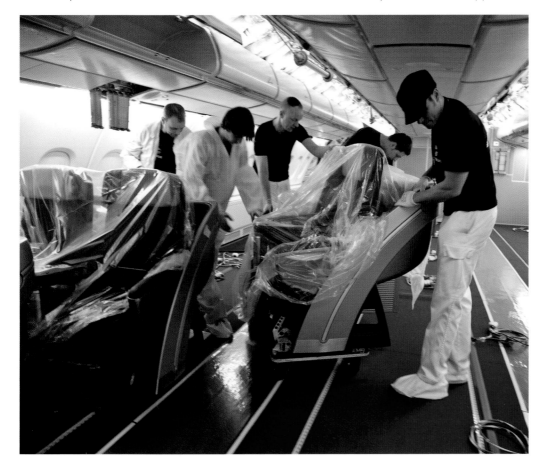

LEFT A cabin fit-out crew prepare the economy cabin on this A380 in Hamburg. *(Airbus)*

main and cargo decks. Non-textile flooring is installed, as well as the forward stairs (the rear stairs are installed in Toulouse), followed by the galley lift and sidewall panels. Next come the galleys, the lavatories and overhead luggage compartments.

Production teams work to strict schedules given that all the components needed in the cabin arrive on a just-in-time basis, an inventory strategy employed by Airbus to increase efficiency and decrease waste by receiving the various items only as they are needed in the production process, thereby reducing inventory and storage costs.

Cabin doors are fitted next, as are passenger necessities including lighting and oxygen masks. The next team is on hand to install the

carpets, ceiling panels and, of course, the seats in their various configurations.

The final part of the jigsaw puzzle comes in the form of the cabin systems (used by the crew for passenger announcements and communication with one another) as well as the complex in-flight entertainment system in each seat.

All the installed items are then thoroughly tested and inspected ahead of a visit by the customer airline. Chapter 6 explains more about cabin design and development.

Painting

Following final assembly in Toulouse, the empty and unpainted A380s are flown to Finkenwerder in Hamburg where they are

painted in one of the two high-tech A380 paint shops before final delivery. The paint shop has a sophisticated ventilation system and a multitude of heat exchangers that capture over 70% of the thermal energy for recycling.

The 'green jets' arrive with their tails and engines already painted, requiring only the wings and fuselage to be painted. These arrive with a layer of anti-corrosive protection, hence the colour and name. First the plane's outer surfaces are sanded and cleaned, then landing gear, antennas, doors and windows are all covered with impermeable protective sheeting and masking tape before the first coat, a chromate-free primer, is applied.

There are different ways of painting the aircraft, but typically up to 24 masked painters move around the aircraft on hovering tele-platforms, applying around 3,600 litres of paint to cover the 3,100m² exterior surface. They spray back and forth like table tennis players in slow motion from a distance of about 30cm.

Next comes an intermediate coat that will enable ecological removal of the upper coats every eight to ten years. This is followed by a layer of the customer's primary colour choice.

Once the super jumbo is dry, marking film that has already been cut to size is put in place and the aircraft's registration lettering is sprayed on. The aircraft is not de-masked until the final coats are dry. Two clear top coats are then applied, sprayed on by hand, taking 24 hours to dry. The finished five-layer paint job is a mere 0.2mm thick and adds around 650kg of weight to the aircraft –

LEFT Work crews mask out the Qatar logo on the underside of the fuselage before painting can begin. *(Airbus)*

CENTRE This Qatar A380 receives its colours – movable roof-mounted tele-platforms enable the paint team to access all areas of the giant double-decker with ease. *(Airbus)*

amazingly little for an aircraft of this size and a big fuel-saving factor, too.

Painting an A380 can take up to two weeks, depending on the complexity of the colour scheme.

Delivery

Final acceptance and delivery of A380s for customers in Europe and the Middle East takes place from the Jürgen Thomas Delivery Centre in Hamburg. The facility bears the name of the former head of Airbus's Large Aircraft Division, who was in charge of the development of the aircraft programme between 1996 and 2001.

The process of handover typically takes a week and involves a customer delegation of specialists, including a pilot, structural engineer, avionics specialist and an airworthiness representative reviewing the aircraft prior to acceptance. A customer acceptance flight is customary and this is followed by what is known as Technical Acceptance Completion (TAC).

Any outstanding documentation (including the bill of sale) are then completed and any final payments are made by the airline to Airbus before ownership is transferred.

The delivery centre, opened in July 2008, conveniently enables Airbus to perform the entire process of aircraft delivery in one place, including aircraft and cabin inspection, as well as all legal and administrative processes.

LEFT The distinctive British Airways tail graphics – and those of all other A380 airlines – are painted in Stade, Germany, rather than at Toulouse. *(Airbus)*

LEFT The initial British Airways A380 breaks cover for the first time in Hamburg before flying to Heathrow. *(Airbus)*

BELOW Job done! An elated paint crew provide a send-off for this British Airways A380. *(Airbus)*

CHAPTER 4

Engines

OPPOSITE The Rolls-Royce Trent 900 has proved to be the more popular engine variant for the A380 with nine customers making use of the British-made powerplant. *(Rolls-Royce)*

Introduction

Two manufacturers offer alternative engine options for the A380 – Rolls-Royce and Engine Alliance (EA).

The former is a major manufacturer of aero engines for all sectors of the aviation market. Its engines power more than 35 types of commercial aircraft and the company has more than 13,000 engines in service around the world. The latter features two of the aviation industry's biggest hitters in the form of a joint venture between General Electric and Pratt & Whitney.

Airbus had initially intended to make use of existing engines available in the market but as the super jumbo concept took shape, it was apparent that a new, more powerful engine would be needed. Both manufacturers were faced with the challenge of delivering the thrust needed to get the aircraft airborne, but at the same time had to respect the latest environmental standards imposed on the aviation industry.

Although Rolls-Royce was selected as the engine for A380 launch customer Singapore Airlines, EA formed strong ties with Emirates, securing them a leading position. At the same time, Rolls-Royce established a wider customer base across more airlines flying the A380. Both engines have proved up to the task with various upgrades making them more appealing. By late 2016 Rolls-Royce had gained more than 50% market share on the aircraft, in addition to being selected by the majority of A380 customers after winning its largest ever order to provide Trent 900 engines and support services to Emirates.

This chapter offers insight into the two manufacturers and how both continue to improve the efficiency and durability of their respective products through advances in technology.

RIGHT Launch customer, Singapore Airlines, decided early on their initial order for 10 A380s would be powered by the Trent 900. *(Rolls-Royce)*

Rolls-Royce Trent 900

Once Airbus had formally announced the commencement of the A380 project, Rolls-Royce felt there was sufficient scope to commence development of what would become known as the Trent 900. As early as October 2000, the engine was chosen by launch customer, Singapore Airlines, for its order of ten A380s and this was quickly followed by Qantas four months later.

The Trent 900 is a high bypass ratio, triple spool turbofan engine, developed from the Rolls-Royce RB211 and is one of the leading products in the wider Trent family. The engine made its maiden flight on 17 May 2004, using Airbus's A340-300 testbed. Final certification was granted by the EASA five months later in Europe and approval was given after two years by the FAA. The engine differs from other large turbofan engines by having three spools. The addition of an intermediate pressure spool adds weight but its inclusion improves efficiency and ensures the engine is competitive in performance with two-spool designs.

RIGHT The Trent 900 is a high-bypass ratio turbofan engine, its distinguishing feature being that it is also a triple-spool engine (the fan is separated from the low-pressure compressor and turbine, thus creating three spools). (Lufthansa)

Initial production delays of the A380 forced a 12-month suspension in engine manufacturing by Rolls-Royce, but the order book soon boomed as British Airways announced the selection of the Trent 900 to power its 12 A380 aircraft, helping to take the engine's share of the A380 engine market to 52% by early 2009.

Demand for the Trent 900 has been strong, given its environmental performance (fuel-burn,

LEFT Rolls-Royce recently secured its largest order in a mega-deal with Emirates for more than 200 engines. *(Rolls-Royce)*

RIGHT The Trent 900's 24 fan blades are hollow, titanium wide-chord blades and the product of decades of finessing and collaboration. The fan blades play a hugely important role in an engine and, together, they draw a tonne of air per second into the engine to produce 80% of the required thrust. Titanium is the chosen material because it's sturdy, lightweight and resistant to damage from foreign objects. To make the fan blades exceptionally fuel-efficient, Rolls-Royce have introduced a unique, patented pattern that also makes them light and aerodynamic. *(Rolls-Royce)*

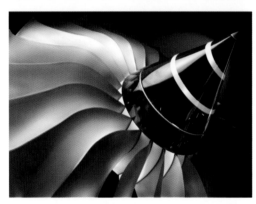

noise, emissions and weight) together with the fact that the engine is certified at additional thrust ratings, demonstrating the growth capability embedded in the engine should further aircraft development be required.

The Trent 900's 24 fan blades feature a swept design that reduces the effect of shock waves; the tip of the fan rotates supersonically, making it lighter, quieter and more efficient than earlier engines. The fan containment system is the first to be manufactured from titanium and at the core of the engine, the high-pressure shaft rotates in the opposite direction to the two other shafts, meaning the engine can be made lighter and more fuel efficient.

In a major upset, Rolls-Royce won the Emirates order of more than 200 engines to power 50 Airbus A380s ordered in late 2013, displacing Engine Alliance which had been the sole supplier to the airline. The decision by Emirates to go with Rolls-Royce had been driven by the manufacturer's willingness to improve reliability and inject technology from the Trent 1000 (developed for the Boeing 787) and the Trent XWB (developed for the Airbus A350). As the fourth generation of the Trent family of engines, the Trent 900 benefits from the manufacturer's ability to feed back low-risk new technology from future generations. These have come in the form of enhanced performance (EP) packages for both in-service and new-build Trent 900s.

Ahead of the first Emirates aircraft being delivered with the Trent 900, the airline identified what it called 'performance problems' which needed to be resolved. The issue was related to the engine's ability to deal with the rigours of Dubai's high temperatures and dusty climate, with the Trent 900 at risk of additional wear and tear against EA's GP7200. Understandably, Emirates wanted to avoid unnecessary downtime and even though maintenance would be at the engine maker's expense, taking an A380 out of service is hugely disruptive to flight planning schedules.

Technical specifications

First flight	May 2004
Type	Three-shaft high bypass ratio (8.7–8.5) turbofan engine
Length	5,478mm (215.7in) tip of spinner minus rubber tip to tail bearing housing plug mount flange
Diameter	2,950mm (116in) fan
Dry weight	6,246kg (13,770lb)
Components	
Compressor	Single-stage LP (fan), 8-stage IP compressor (IPC), 6-stage HP compressor (HPC)
Combustors	Single annular combustor
Turbine	Single-stage HP turbine (HPT), single-stage IP turbine (IPT), 5-stage LP turbine (LPT)
Performance	
Maximum thrust	344–357kN or 77,000–80,000lbf
Overall pressure ratio	37–39
Thrust-to-weight ratio	5.46–6.11 (assuming 6,246kg (13,770lb) mass/weight of engine and certified to 334–374kN or 75,000–84,000lbf of thrust)
Cost	Estimated at £10 million per engine excluding service package

A fix was agreed and both parties were no doubt pleased to have resolved matters as Emirates started taking delivery of 25 Rolls-powered A380s in early 2017.

The delivery of the initial four Trent 900 engines to Airbus for installation on the first of Emirates' 52 A380s was significant as it made the Trent 900 the engine of choice, both in terms of number of customers and also in terms of overall market share.

The delivery was also significant in that Emirates' Trent 900s are the first to be built to the new enhanced performance (EP3) standard. The EP3 package, which is the current build standard at the time of writing, includes elliptical leading edges on compressor blades, and a variety of improvements in the internal aerodynamics of the engine, all contributing towards enhanced fuel economy and improved longevity before maintenance is required.

Key components

The principal modules of the engine are:

- Low-pressure compressor (LPC) rotor
- Intermediate-pressure (IP) compressor
- Intermediate case
- HP system (this includes the high-pressure compressor (HPC), the combustion system and the high-pressure turbine (HPT))
- IP turbine
- External gearbox
- LPC case
- Low-pressure turbine (LPT).

The IP and LPC/LPT assemblies turn in a counter-clockwise direction and the HPC/HPT assembly turns in a clockwise direction (when seen from the rear of the engine) during engine operation.

The compressors increase the pressure of the air, which flows through the engine. The necessary power to turn the compressors is supplied by turbines.

LEFT A Rolls-Royce Trent 900 undergoes a routine check at the British Airways maintenance facility at Heathrow. (Author)

QANTAS FLIGHT QF32

On 4 November 2010, while climbing through 7,000ft after departing from Changi Airport, Singapore, a Trent-powered Airbus A380, VH-OQA, with 469 people on board sustained an uncontained engine rotor failure (UERF) of the No. 2 engine. Debris from the UERF impacted the aircraft, resulting in significant structural and systems damage.

The experienced flight crew, led by Captain Richard de Crespigny, managed to land the crippled aircraft and safely disembark the passengers. 'The sound of the engine failure was really like a backfire in a car – like a boom – so that is something we just react to instinctively with procedures that we learn in the simulator,' he said following the incident. 'A second boom, however, about half a second later, was unusual. It brought up questions of whether one or two engines had been affected and how severe the damage was. [. . .] What you have to do is fly the aeroplane; you have to aviate. There's no fight or flight syndrome,' he added. Qantas grounded its fleet of six A380s for more than three weeks after the accident pending the investigation.

The Australian Transport Safety Bureau (ATSB) found that a number of oil feed stub pipes within the HP/IP hub assembly were manufactured with thin wall sections that did not conform to the design specifications. These non-conforming pipes were fitted to Trent 900 engines, including the No. 2 engine on VH-OQA. The thin wall section significantly reduced the life of the oil feed stub pipe on the No. 2 engine so that a fatigue crack developed, ultimately releasing oil during the flight that resulted in an internal oil fire. That fire led to the separation of the IP turbine disc from the driveshaft. The disc accelerated and burst with sufficient force that the engine structure could not contain it, releasing high-energy debris.

The aircraft was repaired at an estimated cost of £85m and was fitted with four new engines as well as a repaired left wing. Before returning to service on 28 April 2012, the aircraft had extensive on-ground testing and two test flights.

(Rolando Ugolini)

The LP system has a one-stage compressor installed at the front of the engine. A shaft connects the single-stage LPC to a five-stage axial flow turbine at the rear of the gas generator. The gas generator also includes an eight-stage IP compressor, a six-stage HPC and a combustion system.

Each of the compressors in the gas generator is connected to, and turned by, a different turbine. Between the HPC and the HPT is the annular combustion system that burns a mixture of fuel and air to supply energy as heat. Behind the LPT there is a collector nozzle assembly through which the hot gas exhaust flows.

Engine Alliance GP7200

Established in 1996 to develop, manufacture, sell and support a family of advanced technology engines for new high-capacity, long-range aircraft, Engine Alliance is a Connecticut-based joint venture between two giants of the aviation industry – General Electric Aviation and Pratt & Whitney (P&W). Their combined expertise resulted in what is today known as the GP7200.

The GP7200 was derived from two of the most successful wide-body engines in aviation history – the GE90 and the PW4000. Both of these engines had demonstrated industry-

BELOW Emirates is the only airline to fly A380s powered by both Engine Alliance and Rolls-Royce. *(Engine Alliance)*

leading reliability and formed the basis of the new engine, combining the GE90 core and the PW4000 low-spool heritage, with a responsible infusion of new technologies. The engine was originally intended to power Boeing's 747-500X and 600X projects that were announced at the 1996 Farnborough Air Show.

The proposed models would have combined the 747's fuselage with a new wing derived from the 777 to cope with a larger fuselage and increased number of passengers. Boeing intended adding more powerful engines but the overall project cost – estimated to be in the region of £3.9 billion – deterred possible investors and the manufacturer was not able to attract enough interest from airlines. There was only one alternative for Engine Alliance – to put its product forward as the preferred choice for the Airbus A380 super jumbo.

Ground testing of the engine began in April 2004 and was first flight tested as the No. 2 engine on GE's 747 flying testbed in December 2004. It received American Federal Aviation Administration (FAA) certification for commercial operation two years later. Ground tests on an A380 commenced in August 2006 and just weeks later the first flight of an Engine Alliance-powered A380 took place from Toulouse. Final assembly of the GP7200 takes place at Pratt & Whitney's facility in Connecticut.

Approval for certification is understandably a rigorous affair, including everything from fan blade-out containment to bird and water ingestion, icing, in-flight performance and lengthy endurance testing whereby engines accumulate more than 15,000 'service-ready' cycles. Included in the testing was an extended twin-engine operation performance standards (ETOPS) ground demonstration to showcase the engine's reliability. ETOPS is the aviation industry's set of rules that enhance safety when flying over areas of the world that have few airports that can be used in an emergency.

Although the competing Rolls-Royce Trent 900 was named as the lead engine for the project back in 1996 and was initially selected by almost all A380 customers, the GP7200 secured a massive share of the market courtesy of a single transaction when Emirates Airlines ordered 55 engines for its fleet.

The engine's 24-blade fan (manufactured by P&W) is specifically designed to meet Heathrow's stringent noise requirements. The engine is seen as very reliable and was chosen by the likes of Air France and Korean Air to power their A380s.

In 2011 an upgrade was announced which led to a cut in weight for each engine by 23kg

(51lb). Other improvements have included upgrades to improve durability performance, particularly for operations in the Middle East, where the harsh climate also presents challenges for the GP7200 in the searing heat and dust. There has been much discussion about a possible (final) upgrade to the GP7200 by Engine Alliance for the A380, but clearly this would depend on demand for the engine and a clear business plan to justify the further investment needed.

Technical specifications

First flight	December 2004
Type	Two-spool high-bypass axial turbofan engine
Length	4.74m (15.6ft; 187in)
Diameter	3.16m (10.4ft; 124in), fan tip 2.95m (9.7ft; 116in)
Dry weight	6,712kg (14,797lb)
Components	
Compressor	24 swept wide-chord hollow titanium fan blades, 8.7:1 bypass ratio; five-stage low-pressure axial compressor; nine-stage high-pressure axial compressor
Combustors	Low-emissions single annular combustor
Turbine	Two-stage high-pressure turbine, boltless architecture, single crystal blades, split-blade cooling and thermal barrier coatings, axial flow; six-stage low-pressure axial flow
Performance	
Maximum thrust	363kN, 81,500lbf, 36,980kgf
Overall pressure ratio	43.9
Thrust-to-weight ratio	5.508 (assuming 14,797lbf weight of engine and 81,500lbf of thrust)
Cost	Estimated at £10 million per engine excluding service package

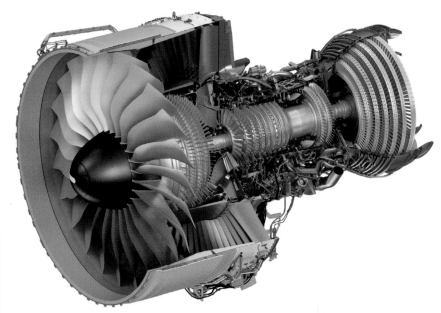

ABOVE The GP7200 features 24 swept wide-chord hollow titanium fan blades and a five-stage low-pressure axial compressor.
(Engine Alliance)

Key components

The GP7200 has four major sections: the compressor section, combustion section, turbine section and the accessory drive section.

The compressor section supplies high-pressure (HP) compressed air to the diffuser/burner for core engine thrust, aircraft service bleed systems and bypass air for thrust. A five-stage low-pressure (LP) compressor rotor assembly is located to the rear of the fan rotor. An acoustic splitter fairing directs the primary airstream into the nine-stage HP compressor rotor assembly.

The HP compressor has three stages of

variable inlet guide vanes (IGVs) and external bleeds from stages four, seven and nine, with an internal bleed from stage six.

The combustion section receives compressed heated air from the HP compressor and fuel from the fuel nozzles. The mixture of hot air and fuel is ignited and burned in the single-annular combustion chamber to generate a HP stream of hot gas to turn the HP turbine and LP turbine.

The turbine section consists of HP turbine and LP turbine. The two-stage HP turbine rotor assembly receives the hot gas from the diffuser/burner. The HP turbine supplies the power to turn the HP compressor. The six-stage LP turbine has an active clearance control system for more efficient engine operation. The LP turbine provides the power to turn the LP compressor and fan rotor. The turbine exhaust case (TEC) assembly supplies the structural support for the rear of the engine. The TEC straightens the exhaust gas flow as it exits the engine.

The accessory drive section consists of main gearbox (MGB) and angle gearbox (AGB). The MGB supplies the power to turn the attached engine and aircraft accessories. The AGB transmits the power from the engine rotor to the MGB. During engine start, the AGB transmits the power from the MGB to turn the engine rotor.

The LP rotor system is independent of the HP rotor system. The LP rotor system consists of the LP compressor and the LP turbine. The HP rotor system consists of the HP compressor and the HP turbine.

FADEC

The A380's engines make use of a Full Authority Digital Engine (or Electronics) Control (FADEC) system designed to provide optimum engine efficiency for a given flight condition. It consists primarily of a digital computer – called an electronic engine controller (EEC) or engine control unit (ECU) that controls all aspects of engine performance.

True full authority digital engine controls have no form of manual override available, placing full authority over the operating parameters of the engine in the hands of the computer.

The system works by receiving multiple input variables of the current flying conditions including air density, throttle lever position, engine temperatures, engine pressures and a host of other parameters. It governs engine fuel flow, controls variable engine geometries and even interfaces with the engine thrust reverser. The inputs are received by the EEC and analysed up to 70 times per second. Engine operating parameters such as fuel flow, stator vane position, bleed valve position and others are computed from this data and applied as appropriate. FADEC also controls engine starting and restarting. FADEC not only provides for efficient engine operation, it also allows the manufacturer to program engine limitations and receive engine health and maintenance

AIRLINE ENGINE CHOICES

Rolls-Royce	Engine Alliance
Emirates*	Emirates*
Singapore Airlines	Air France
Qantas	Korean Air
Lufthansa	Qatar Airways
China Southern Airlines	Etihad Airways
Malaysia Airlines	
Thai Airways	
British Airways	
Asiana Airlines	

* Emirates are the only airline to operate A380 aircraft with both engine variants.

BELOW Air France also opted for their A380 fleet to be powered by the Engine Alliance GP7200. (Air France)

reports. For example, to avoid exceeding a certain engine temperature, the FADEC can be programmed to automatically take the necessary measures without pilot intervention.

Advanced features of the FADEC system produced by BAE Systems for the GP7200 include electronic engine overspeed protection, variable engine geometry control and a data transmission system.

Thrust reversers

Airbus initially felt the A380 could be equipped with sufficient braking capacity without the need for thrust reversers, but late on in the development process the manufacturer elected to fit the two inboard engines with reversers. Simply put, thrust reversers allow for the temporary diversion of the aircraft engine's exhaust forward, rather than backwards. This reverse thrust acts against the forward travel of the aircraft, providing deceleration, reducing wear on the brakes and enabling shorter landing distances. They are useful in the deceleration process if water or snow makes the runway slippery.

The thrust reverser assembly closes the engine core with an aerodynamic flow path and uses the outer cowl to make a fan exhaust duct and nozzle exit. The reversers fitted to the A380 are electrically actuated, offering better reliability than their pneumatic or hydraulic equivalents, in addition to saving weight. The A380's two outboard engines do not have reversers, thereby lowering the chance that those engines – which sometimes

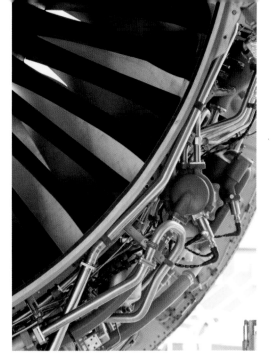

hang over runway edges – might be damaged by ingesting foreign objects.

On the A380, a pilot can deploy the thrust reversers only on the ground, and can select a range of thrust reversal from idle to maximum reverse, until the aircraft has slowed to below 70kts, or 80.5mph (1kt = 1.15mph). At that point, the thrust reversers must be set at idle reverse.

Auxiliary power unit (APU)

The A380's APU is the Pratt & Whitney 980A, the largest APU in commercial airline service. Manufactured in Canada, it is a two-shaft gas turbine engine, specifically designed for the A380. During on-ground operation, it provides bleed air for cabin conditioning from a low spool-driven load compressor, main engine start capability and electrical power from two gearbox-mounted,

120kVA generators. The APU is also designed to deliver in-flight backup power.

The APU also provides compressed air to power the analysis ground station (AGS) on the ground and to start the engines. The AGS is a semi-automatic analysis system of flight data that helps to optimise management of maintenance and reduce costs.

The APU also powers electric generators that provide auxiliary electric power to the aircraft.

RIGHT The APU is located in the tail cone, inside a fireproof compartment. *(Author)*

Primary APU controls and indications are installed in the cockpit, mainly in the overhead panel, centre pedestal panel and forward centre panel. Additionally, two external emergency shut-off controls are installed on the NLG panel and on the refuel/defuel panel.

The APU is installed in the tail cone, in the rear of the fuselage inside a fireproof compartment, with the exhaust muffler located at the end of the tail cone.

Engine health management (EHM)

All A380 engines are equipped with EHM tools that are used to cut the cost of unscheduled maintenance, unnecessary inspection and troubleshooting. Use of the system allows the A380 to benefit from improved operating economics and performance; when an aircraft's engines run cleanly because they are well maintained, fuel bills go down and environmental damage is minimised.

Rolls-Royce, for example, uses EHM to track the health of thousands of its engines operating worldwide – including all those powering the Airbus A380 – using onboard sensors and live satellite feeds.

EHM is a proactive technique for predicting when something might go wrong and averting a potential threat before it has a chance to develop into a real problem. EHM covers the assessment of an engine's state of health in real time or post-flight. Essentially, EHM is about making more informed decisions regarding operating an engine fleet by acting on the best information available.

EHM uses a range of sensors strategically positioned throughout the engine to record key technical parameters several times each flight. The EHM sensors monitor numerous critical engine characteristics such as temperatures, pressures, speeds, flows and vibration levels to ensure they are within known tolerances and to highlight when they are not. In the most extreme cases aircrew could be contacted, but far more often the action will fall to the airline's maintenance personnel or a Rolls-Royce service representative in the field to manage a special service inspection.

The Trent 900 engine can be fitted

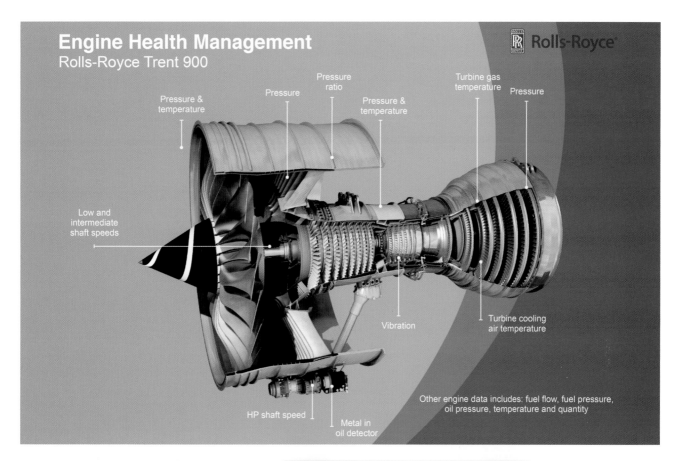

Engine Health Management
Rolls-Royce Trent 900

Rolls-Royce

Pressure & temperature

Pressure

Pressure ratio

Pressure & temperature

Turbine gas temperature

Pressure

Low and intermediate shaft speeds

Vibration

Turbine cooling air temperature

HP shaft speed

Metal in oil detector

Other engine data includes: fuel flow, fuel pressure, oil pressure, temperature and quantity

permanently with around 25 sensors. Many of these are multi-purpose as they are used to control the engine and provide an indication of engine operation to the pilots as well as being used by the EHM system.

The main engine parameters – shaft speeds and turbine gas temperature – are used to give a clear view of the overall health of the engine. A number of pressure and temperature sensors are fitted through the gas path of the engine to enable the performance of each of the main modules (including the fan, the intermediate- and high-pressure compressors and the high-, intermediate- and low-pressure turbines) to be calculated. These sensors are fitted between each module, except where the temperature is too high for reliable measurements to be made.

Vibration sensors provide valuable information on the condition of all the rotating components. An electric magnetic chip detector is fitted to trap any debris in the oil system that may be caused by unusual wear to bearings or gears. Other sensors are used to assess the health of the fuel system, the oil system and the cooling air system.

ABOVE Engine Health Management is used to identify issues in an engine well in advance – this helps to cut the cost of maintenance and greatly assists in improved operating economics. *(Author)*

LEFT Sensors in the engine provide valuable information to airline engineers on the ground so that any potential problems can be dealt with expeditiously. *(Author)*

CHAPTER 5

Flight deck and systems

OPPOSITE The A380's state-of-the-art glass cockpit and fly-by-wire system has enabled flight crews to embrace new technology and to interact with the aircraft in new ways. *(Airbus)*

Introduction

The A380's cockpit – based on Airbus's industry-leading flight deck design for its fly-by-wire family of aircraft – features the latest advances in cockpit technology, including larger interactive displays and an advanced flight management system.

Flight crews have embraced the new technology and the way in which it allows them to interact with the aircraft. The fly-by-wire system is praised by pilots for the similarity in handling qualities it offers whether flying an aircraft with a take-off weight of 50 or 575 tonnes.

In developing the A380 flight deck, Airbus used similar cockpit layout, procedures and handling characteristics to other Airbus aircraft. This has meant the design is familiar to pilots, which has in turn reduced crew training costs as well as maintenance and operational costs.

The cockpit features a clean and minimalist design, more akin to a spaceship than a commercial airliner. The so-called glass cockpit's electronic displays showing flight information are a stand-out feature and pilots have foldable keyboards and trackballs for using the aircraft's computer.

From an avionics perspective, the A380 makes use of an architecture first used in advanced military aircraft, such as the Lockheed Martin F-22 Raptor. The suite is a technological innovation, with networked computing modules to support different applications. The system was designed to minimise latency and reduce the amount of wiring required.

This chapter takes a closer look at the anatomy of the flight deck, the concept of a 'paperless cockpit', flight controls and the complex array of systems – everything from electrics, to oxygen, smoke detection and flight guidance – to provide insight and understanding of what it's like to fly the super jumbo.

EXTERNAL TAXI AID CAMERA SYSTEM

The A380's external taxi aid camera system (ETACS) streams live pictures from external cameras mounted under the nose and on the tailfin and the resulting imagery can be displayed on one of the interactive displays.

The ETACS can assist the flight crew during pushback by allowing them to see and check that the tow truck is connected, that the aircraft's environment is clear of obstacles, and that the groundcrew personnel are in the appropriate positions.

The imagery also assists the pilots in navigating the gigantic aircraft around airport taxiways. The feed is also provided to passengers through the entertainment system to enhance the flight experience.

The system is certainly beneficial; however, looking out of the cockpit window remains the primary means of determining when to initiate turns, and of verifying the aircraft's position relative to the ground track.

Cockpit anatomy

The A380 flight deck is a truly impressive sight, best described as a state-of-the-art 'glass cockpit'. Located in between the main and upper deck, it is accessible via the main deck by the cockpit stairs.

Once inside, the cockpit offers seating for a Captain and First Officer, as well as a third observer seat. A fourth and fifth (optional) occupant folding seat can be included if required.

The cockpit contains the following instrument panels, each of which are described in further detail in the following pages:

■ Overhead panel
■ Main instrument panel
■ Glareshield
■ Pedestal.

The Captain and First Officer both have lateral consoles, each with a sidestick, steering

ABOVE A380 pilots are unanimous in their praise of the paperless cockpit concept, enabling a switch from paper manuals to electronic equivalents of the FCOM (Flight Crew Operating Manual) and MEL (Minimum Equipment List). *(Author)*

THE PAPERLESS COCKPIT

One of the key features on the A380 is its paperless cockpit, designed to reduce the amount of clutter contributed to by reams of flight maps, charts and manuals. This 'electronic library' largely replaces the traditional paper documentation used by pilots and allows flight and maintenance crews to easily locate and display relevant operational information including flight manuals, equipment lists, navigation charts, performance calculations and even the aircraft's logbook.

Aboard the A380, all these documents have been replaced with the network systems server (NSS), converting all necessary information into electronic documents that are then aggregated into the server for instant access whenever they are required.

The NSS connects to the multi-function displays, allowing either pilot to bring up information, such as navigation charts, equipment lists or performance calculations on to one of the displays, rather than sift through documents to find relevant information.

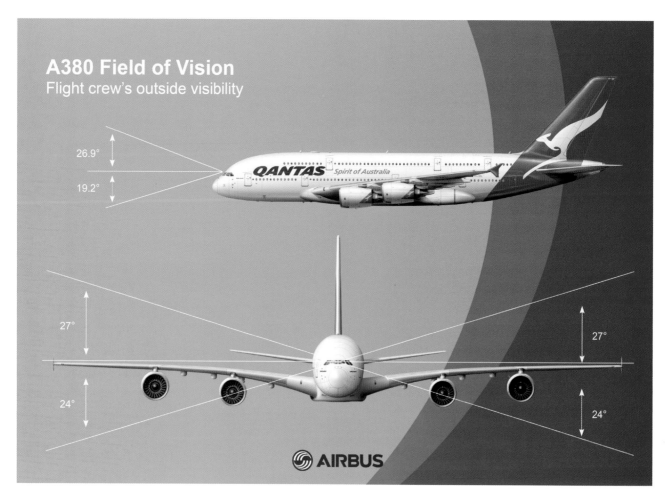

A380 Field of Vision
Flight crew's outside visibility

26.9°
19.2°

27°
27°

24°
24°

AIRBUS

handwheel and oxygen masks. Behind their seats is the folding seat where maintenance staff can access the onboard maintenance terminal (OMT) during the turnround process. In the cockpit floor is a small hatch, used to access the main avionics bay.

An optional flight crew rest compartment can be installed on the main deck just behind the flight deck. This is divided into two separate flight crew compartments, one on top of the other. The entrance to the lower compartment is on the main deck at the rear wall of the compartment, while the entrance to the upper compartment is at the top of the cockpit stairs.

Field of vision

Any flight crew's field of vision – or vision envelope as it is sometimes called – is determined by the layout of the cockpit, the shape of the nose cone, the windshield and the side window panels. When it comes to

the A380, these have been designed to obtain an outside visibility comparable to that of any other modern aircraft, and in many respects the visibility is greater than that defined by the relevant aerospace standards.

Main instrument panel

Almost certainly the most noticeable innovation in the Airbus A380 cockpit has been the introduction of eight interchangeable liquid crystal displays. These consist of the following, all of which can be customised to cater to the pilot's preference:

■ Two primary flight displays (PFD)
■ Two navigation displays (ND)
■ One engine/warning display (E/WD)
■ One system display (SD)
■ Two multi-function displays (MFD).

The eight-screen display replaces the previous method of using three multi-function control

RIGHT Schematics generated on the cockpit LCDs provide the flight crew with a wealth of information on the likes of the fuel system tank arrangement (top), movement of control surfaces (middle) and cabin pressure (bottom). In the upper image, the valves are shown as green circles and the tanks as square boxes, with the four engines displayed at the top. *(Author)*

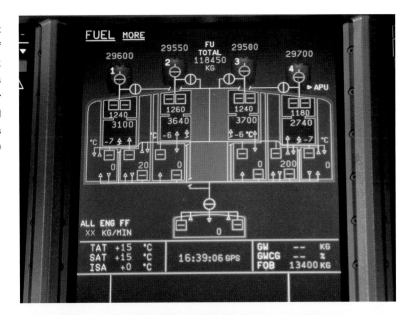

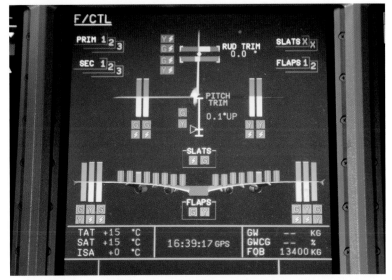

and display units, with the screens placed around the pilot's eye line. Multi-function displays are of particular interest, as they play a vital role in hosting the information stored in the NSS, which stores all flight information. The MFDs provide an easy-to-use interface to the flight management system – replacing three multi-function control and display units. They include QWERTY keyboards and trackballs, interfacing with a graphical 'point-and-click' display navigation system; combined, this is called the keyboard and cursor control unit (KCCU).

The main instrument panel also includes:

- Two onboard information terminals (OIT), each with associated additional keys and a keyboard and pointing device integrated in the sliding table. The OIT is the flight crew's interface with the onboard information system (OIS) applications.
- Two integrated standby instrument systems (ISIS) for backup navigation.

At 15cm × 20cm each, their increased display size provides improved situational awareness for pilots, and allows for such enhanced presentation modes as a vertical situation awareness function that presents a 'vertical cut' of the aircraft trajectory incorporating flight path, terrain and weather information.

The increased screen space also allows the pilots to make use of moving airport maps,

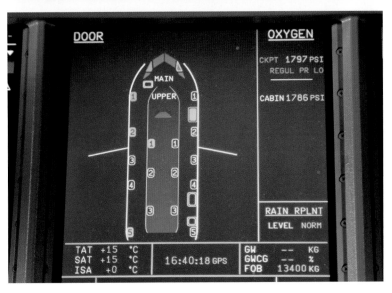

RIGHT The central Engine/Warning Display is one of eight interchangeable LCD displays. *(Author)*

BELOW The anatomy of the A380 cockpit. *(Airbus/Author)*

Overhead Panel

Glareshield

Main Instrument Panel

Captain's Seat

First Officer's Seat

Pedestal

consisting of detailed layouts of common airport destinations, allowing safer ground taxi operations.

Glareshield

The glareshield is located just below the windscreen and above the main instrument panel and houses the automatic flight controls such as the autopilot. In the A380 the glareshield includes:

■ One flight control unit (FCU) with:
   ♦ Two electronic flight instrument system control panels (EFIS CP) – each EFIS CP is used to select the display on the onside primary flight display (PFD) and navigation display (ND), and to change the barometer settings.
   ♦ One auto flight system control panel (AFS CP) – the AFS CP is the main interface with the flight guidance (FG) system.
■ Two panels with:
   ♦ Attention getters: master warning and master caution lights
   ♦ Sidestick priority lights
   ♦ Autoland lights.

The glareshield also contains two panels with loudspeaker sound level controls and air traffic control (ATC) message indicators.

LEFT The glareshield houses the automatic flight controls such as the autopilot. *(Author)*

BELOW The A380's thrust levers sit in the centre of the pedestal, flanked by the Keyboard and Cursor Control Units. *(Author)*

Pedestal

The central pedestal is positioned between the seats of the Captain and First Officer. It includes:

- Two KCCUs, used to interface with the SD and its onside MFD and ND.
- Two radio management panels (RMPs) – these are used to tune all radio communications, enter the squawk code, adjust the volume for communication and NAVAID identification and also act as backup for radio navigation.
- One SURV control panel – this is used to interface with the SURVeillance (SURV) functions of the aircraft, including the terrain awareness and warning system (TAWS), weather radar and traffic collision avoidance system (TCAS).
- One ECAM control panel (ECP) – this is the interface with the electronic centralised aircraft monitoring (ECAM).
- Thrust levers and engine master levers.
- The pedestal also includes panels for the following flight controls: pitch trim and rudder trim panels, speed brake lever and flaps/slats lever, as well as the parking brake panel.

ABOVE The overhead panel is used to manage several key aircraft systems, including fire, hydraulics, air and engine starting. *(Airbus)*

Overhead panel

The overhead panel includes the system controls and is arranged in three main rows. The centre row is for engine-related systems, arranged in a logical way to cover fire, hydraulics, fuel, electrical and air systems, anti-icing, cabin pressure and engine starting. On either side there are two lateral rows for other systems, including the likes of smoke detection, fuel jettison, emergency electrical power and windscreen wiper controls. Either pilot can reach all the controls on the overhead panel.

Flight controls

The A380 features fly-by-wire flight controls, relying on electronic signals to move the aircraft's control surfaces rather than mechanically operated systems of the past. Although the handling similarity is created artificially, the feel of the controls will produce the same result in the A380 as in the relatively tiny A318, even if greater inertia means it will take a little longer for a change in flight trajectory to take place.

Instead of a traditional control column and

LEFT When flying the aircraft manually, the side stick (and rudder pedal) inputs are fed to six flight control computers, which in turn determine the movement of the flight control surfaces. *(Author)*

yoke, A380 pilots have use of a sidestick control located conveniently out of the way to their left (for the Captain) or to their right (for the First Officer). Short and stubby, this controller looks more at home as part of a video console or in a fighter jet, not as the primary input for control of a 575-tonne aircraft.

The flight controls can be divided into two categories – the primary flight controls, which direct the aircraft according to the three axes (roll, pitch and yaw) and fulfil the auxiliary functions, together with the slats and flaps which fulfil the high-lift function.

The A380 introduced several major evolutions when it came to flight controls. The most significant was the fact that all mechanical backup controls were replaced by electrical equivalents. This system is totally segregated from the normal flight control system and relies on the availability of the Green or Yellow hydraulic power source and the use of dedicated sensors and transducers in the pilot controls. The Green hydraulic reservoir is located in pylon 1, above

engine 1 on the left wing and is powered by four engine-driven pumps on engines 1 and 2. The Yellow hydraulic reservoir is located in pylon 4, above engine 4 on the right wing and is powered by four engine-driven pumps on engines 3 and 4.

Other developments included the addition of a new pitch trim switch, designed to replace the trim wheels given the removal of mechanical pitch trim control, integration of the FG and flight envelope (FE) function in the primary flight computers and the introduction of active stability for longitudinal and lateral axes in order to reduce the size of the horizontal and vertical tailplane.

This FE control system retains complete flight control, preventing pilots from flying outside of performance limits. This has allowed Airbus to tailor computer flight control laws, greatly increasing flight safety and decreasing crew workload. The system was cited as a substantial help when a Qantas Airbus A380 suffered a major engine failure over Indonesia, forcing it to return to Singapore (see page 94 for more details on the incident).

BELOW The A380 passes through six distinct flight profile phases. *(Author)*

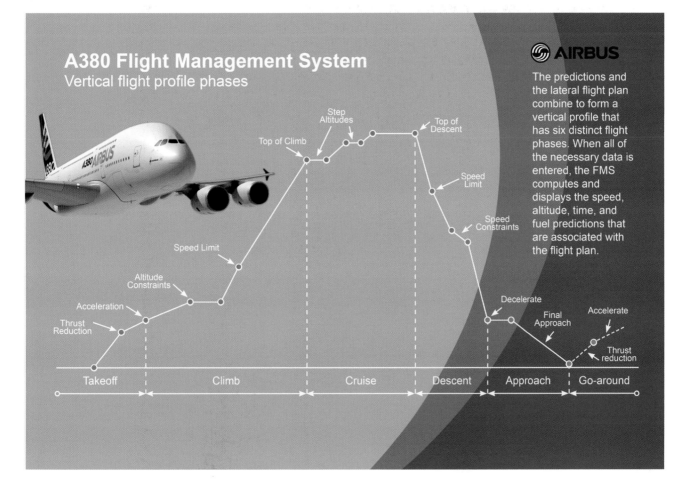

The simulators British Airways uses are housed within the perimeter of Heathrow Airport, alongside the airline's engineering base. The A380 simulator is the latest of 16 which BA uses to train its pilots on all Boeing and Airbus planes operating in its fleet.

With an approximate pricetag of some £12 million, the British Airways A380 simulator is the latest addition to this state-of-the-art facility. Inside the training centre, the simulators are set in a line and look like white domes on stilts, two storeys tall and accessed through retractable gangplanks, allowing space for the motion envelope of each pod.

The simulator is calibrated to operate with the Rolls-Royce Trent 900 engines and operates from a 230/400V, 3-phase, 5-wire, 50/60Hz power supply to support the simulator's motion, visual display, computers and air conditioning requirements. To achieve optimum directivity and realism, six loudspeaker channels are installed in the flight compartment area and handle up to 115dB at full power.

The impressive visual display system comprises a 200° × 40° surround screen and flight deck occupants will view the scene displayed on the back projection screen via the collimating mirror. A 10ft radius concave mirror collimates the image to near-infinity. The large mirror size provides a 54in-wide viewing volume, enabling all flight deck occupants to view the image.

The mirror is formed by stretching an aluminised polyester film over a concave structure of lightweight material. The cavity behind the mirror is partly evacuated so that a continuous concave mirror section is formed. The vacuum is then maintained by an accurate closed loop system.

The motion simulation system, provided by Thales, is a synergistic six-degree of freedom motion system utilising hydrostatic/hydrodynamic actuators with full digital control. The motion system is so advanced that it will respond to a step input within 0.05 seconds.

The simulator uses data gleaned from actual aircraft as well as real cockpit components to make the experience as lifelike as possible. The motion system which moves the simulator gives so-called 'motion cues'. Tipping it slightly tricks the balance systems of the flight deck occupants to convince them they are really moving.

'When you are accelerating it moves the simulator back, so you get pressed back into your seat and when you are decelerating it tips the nose of the simulator down,' says the lead engineer for L3 Link, Simulation and Training, the company which builds the simulators.

Inside the pod is an exact replica of the A380's cockpit, with its countless screens and switches, and once the impressive display system is switched on, it's easy to simply immerse yourself in the simulator and instantly feel like you are on board a real aircraft.

From personal experience – including a take-off and landing back at Heathrow – the simulator looks, feels and performs just like the real deal. So accurate is the detail, that one sees baggage being delivered to the aircraft and the headlights of cars passing around the airport's perimeter road. Any international airport can be loaded and flying conditions set – or even mechanical faults

RIGHT The simulator's virtual display system is projected onto a surround screen with lifelike graphics.
(Author)

LEFT The British Airways simulator's motion system will respond to an input in 0.05 seconds. *(Author)*

introduced – at the touch of a button.

Given that it takes 18 months and £100,000 to train a commercial airline pilot from scratch, the benefits and cost savings provided by the simulator are clear. Pilots can be trained in ways that can never be replicated in a real aircraft, creating unexpected situations. Next time you're flying, bear that in mind. Whatever the real world might throw at them, chances are the pilots have already trained for it.

BELOW The simulators use actual flight data to enhance the training experience. *(Airbus)*

TYPICAL A380 PILOT QUALIFICATIONS

Captain prerequisites

To qualify as an A380 Captain, prospective candidates will have previously qualified on JAR/FAR 25 turbojet aircraft equipped with glass cockpit technology including FMS and commercial operations.

- Valid and current ATPL
- Previous command experience
- Jet experience
- Fluent in English
- Flight time
  - ◆ 1,500 hours as a pilot
  - ◆ 1,000 hours on JAR/FAR 25* aircraft
  - ◆ 200 hours' experience as airline, corporate or military transport pilot.

First officer prerequisites

Prospective First Officers will have previously qualified on JAR/FAR 25 turbojet aircraft equipped with glass cockpit technology including FMS and commercial operations.

- Valid and current CPL with IR
- Jet experience
- Fluent in English
- Flight time
  - ◆ 500 hours as a pilot
  - ◆ 300 hours on JAR/FAR 25 aircraft
  - ◆ 200 hours' experience as airline, corporate or military transport pilot.

Time savings in pilot training from one Airbus type to another lead to lower training costs for airlines and considerably increased crew productivity. The annual savings in training and payroll costs through improved productivity from the reduced transition time can be up to £250,000 per new aircraft added to the fleet.

* JAR refers to Joint Aviation Requirements and FAR refers to Federal Aviation Regulations for large turbine-powered aircraft.

BELOW Airlines have reported that their pilots have coped well with the technical complexity of the A380 flight deck. (Lufthansa)

Head-up-display (HUD)

The A380 offers its pilots the option of an HUD, previously more common in the fighter pilot realm than when it comes to flying commercial aircraft, but a great example of technology transferring over. The system shows critical flight information symbols superimposed on to external visual cues – including the landscape, horizon and runways – in the pilots' forward field of view.

The HUD computer (HUDC) receives data from the aircraft's sensors and generates the display symbology. The head-up projection unit (HPU) includes an LCD imager that projects the image on to the head-up combiner unit (HCU). The HCU is an optical element (essentially a glass plate), mounted between the pilot's head and the windscreen that reflects the projected image towards the pilot. While the superimposed image (to infinity) provides flight information to the pilot, he can continue to see external scenes in a completely normal way (through the HCU's glass plate). A memory module aligns the optical references of the HUD cockpit equipment with those of the aircraft.

The HUD contributes significantly to increasing the pilots' situational awareness, particularly during the approach and landing phases by showing trajectory-related symbols superimposed on the actual external view.

Avionics bays

Interestingly, the A380 has three avionics bays – a main avionics bay, an upper avionics bay and an aft avionics bay.

The main avionics bay contains the normal electrical power centre and most of the systems' computers. This is accessible through a door in the forward cargo hold area, via a hatch from outside, or via a hatch within the cockpit.

The upper bay contains the emergency electrical power centre, some ultimate emergency equipment, the NSS and most of the in-flight entertainment (IFE) equipment. This bay is accessible from the upper deck area, via a door.

The aft bay is a very small, boiler-style closet at the rear of the main deck. It only houses a few electronic control boxes (ECBs) related to the HF

TOP The main avionics bay beneath the cockpit contains most of the aircraft's systems computers. *(Author)*

ABOVE The aircraft's giant nickel-cadmium batteries are located in the upper avionics bay. *(Author)*

LEFT The aircraft's Network Server System (NSS) is the heart of the A380's paperless cockpit. *(Author)*

radio equipment. This makes radio frequency interference design-sense as the HF antenna is located in the leading edge of the vertical stabiliser.

The A380 employs an integrated modular avionics (IMA) architecture, first used in advanced military aircraft, such as the Lockheed Martin F-22 Raptor, Lockheed Martin F-35 Lightning II and Dassault Rafale.

Computer architecture

The A380's computer architecture was chosen to ensure it could take advantage of optimised flight data processing – and the super jumbo has nearly a million parameters that need analysis.

The architecture is based on a system of networked, real-time servers and routers, combined with a central acquisition of parameters and secure digital communications. Although open to the world via digital radio links, the whole onboard system is designed to be highly secure, both from the point of view of computer security and operational availability, thanks to its redundant architecture.

The aircraft's information system collects, centralises and compiles all the data related to the flight on a single system and provides external communication means, data calculation and storage capacities. This modular, central system also hosts applications unique to Airbus and the airlines. The information system is made up of four components that operate in a highly integrated way.

■ Described as the A380's 'central nervous system', the NSS is the system's backbone and the key to the aircraft's unprecedented level of systems integration. The NSS sits at the heart of A380's paperless cockpit.
■ The secure communication interface (SCI) is a link between the aircraft's avionics and the open world. It is designed to guarantee the security of information exchanged between the IFE and the avionics systems, as well as the security of the ground-to-air and air-to-ground exchanges.
■ Designed specifically for A380, the central data acquisition module (CDAM) is a maintenance-monitoring system capable of recording and analysing up to a million parameters. It can generate over a hundred different maintenance reports concerning the maintenance condition of the aircraft and any possible technical failures.
■ The A380 is also equipped with a data loading and configuration system (DLCS) application software for downloading and managing the configuration of onboard computer software.

Key aircraft systems

Pneumatic system	The bleed air system supplies high-pressure air to the following systems: air conditioning and cabin pressurisation, wing and engine anti-ice, engine start, hydraulic reservoir pressurisation and the pack bay ventilation system. In normal conditions, the bleed air system operates automatically. If necessary, it can be manually operated by the pilot.
Air conditioning system	The air conditioning system is fully automatic. It provides continuous air renewal and maintains a constant selected temperature and airflow in the cabin and cockpit zones. Air from the air conditioning system is also used for cargo ventilation. The temperature in the cabin and cockpit can be controlled by the flight crew. The temperature in each cabin zone can be adjusted or directly controlled by the cabin crew. Some air from the cabin is recycled into the bulk cargo compartment for ventilation and temperature regulation (temperature regulation is optional for the forward and aft cargo compartments).
Ventilation system	The aircraft has a fully automatic ventilation system that ventilates the three avionics bays (main, upper and aft), the cockpit and cabin zones, the IFE bay, the pack bays and the bulk and cargo aft compartment. For cabin ventilation, fresh air from the air generation system is mixed with recirculated air from the cabin. This recirculated air is supplied through filters and fans to the mixer unit. Secondary fans recirculate air between the upper and the main deck. The IFE has a fully automatic ventilation system that cools its electronic equipment. The bulk and aft cargo compartments are automatically ventilated. Temperature regulation is possible for the bulk cargo compartment only.

Pressurisation system	In normal operation, the pressurisation system does not require any action by the flight crew. Cabin air pressure is automatically regulated to provide maximum passenger comfort. Cabin pressure regulation is performed via the automatic control of the outflow valves during all flight phases, from take-off to landing. If necessary, the flight crew can manually operate the cabin air pressurisation system by selecting the cabin altitude target and/or the cabin pressure vertical speed. Two independent cabin overboard valves automatically prevent cabin air pressure from going too high or too low, in the event of a pressurisation system failure.
Flight guidance system	The auto flight system (AFS) includes the FG system, which provides short-term lateral and vertical guidance based on flight parameters selected by the flight crew or managed by the FMS. The FMS in turn provides long-term guidance by sending targets to the FG. In order to achieve its objectives, the FG controls the autopilots that provide flight guidance by calculating pitch, roll and yaw orders, the flight directors that display guidance commands on the PFDs – this enables the flight crew to manually fly the aircraft or to monitor the flight guidance orders when the autopilot is engaged, and also the autothrust that controls the thrust of the engines.
Flight management system	The FMS helps flight crews complete flight operation tasks. The flight crew can enter the flight plan into the FMS. This flight plan includes the intended lateral and vertical trajectory. When all of the necessary data is entered, the FMS computes and displays the speed, altitude, time and fuel predictions that are associated with the flight plan. The system provides the following functions: navigation (aircraft position computation, radio navigation tuning, polar navigation), flight planning (flight plan creation, flight plan revisions and flight plan predictions), performance calculation and optimisation, long-term guidance and information display on the MFD, ND and PFD.
Communication system	The A380's communication system enables: External communication: • Radio communication: VHF and HF • Satellite communication: SATCOM • Selective calling (SELCAL). Internal communication: • Flight interphone • Cabin interphone • Passengers' address (PA) • Service interphone.
Electrical system	115V alternating current (AC) power can be provided by three types of power sources: • Engine-driven generators – each engine has one generator. These engine-driven generators are the main source of electrical power. Each can supply up to 150kVA. The A380 uses aluminium power cables instead of copper for weight reduction. • APU generators – the APU can drive two generators. When the APU is running, it drives both generators at the same time. Each APU generator can supply up to 120kVA. • External power units – on the ground, it is possible to connect as many as four external power units. These provide 115V AC power up to 90kVA. The aircraft has four batteries, each with a nominal capacity of 50Ah. These batteries can provide DC power if AC power is not available. In terms of emergency generation, a ram air turbine (RAT) will automatically extend and mechanically drive the emergency generator.
Fire and smoke protection system	The following aircraft zones have a fire detection and extinguishing system: • Engines • APU • Cargo compartments • Lavatories. The following aircraft zones have a fire detection system: • Main landing gear bays • Avionics bays (main, upper and aft bay) • Crew rest compartments. When fire or smoke is detected, the detection is sent to the ECAM in order to trigger an applicable alert.

Hydraulic system	The A380's 350bar (5,000psi) hydraulic system is a significant difference from the typical 210bar (3,000psi) hydraulics used on most commercial aircraft since the 1940s. First used in military aircraft, high-pressure hydraulics reduce the weight and size of pipelines, actuators and related components. The 350bar pressure is generated by eight de-clutchable hydraulic pumps.
	There are two identical and independent hydraulic circuits on board the aircraft – Yellow and Green. They operate continuously and power the flight controls, the landing gear system and the cargo doors. Each hydraulic system is controlled and monitored by its assigned hydraulic system monitoring unit (HSMU). If one or both hydraulic systems fail, the following hydroelectrical backups remain available:
	• For flight controls: the electrical-hydrostatic actuators (EHAs) and the electrical backup hydraulic actuators (EBHAs) • For braking and steering: the local electrohydraulic generation system (LEHGS).
	In terms of hydraulic generation, four engine-driven pumps (two per engine) pressurise each hydraulic system. The pumps of engines 1 and 2 pressurise the Green hydraulic system and the pumps of engines 3 and 4 pressurise the Yellow hydraulic system.
Ice and rain protection system	The ice protection system enables unrestricted operation of the aircraft in icing conditions. This system protects the aircraft against ice by using two methods: hot bleed air for engine anti-ice and wing anti-ice, and electrical power for window heating, water/waste drain masts heating and probe heating. An ice detection system enables the automatic activation and deactivation of the wing and engine anti-ice system, but the flight crew can also manually activate it at any time.
Indicating/recording systems	The following systems and displays – many of which are detailed earlier in the chapter – provide the flight crew with the information necessary to operate the aircraft:
	• Control and display system (CDS) – a display function for flight operation and system operation using eight identical liquid crystal display units (LCDUs) • HUD – provides guidance to the flight crew by gathering primary flight display information • OIS – provides access to flight operation manuals and applications • Clock – this system operates independently of other systems and provides time data to all aircraft systems that require a time and date reference • ISIS – provides information in case of loss of the PFD or ND • Concentrator and multiplexer for video (CMV) – the unit provides treatment and switching of video signals to permit display of various video functions. Inputs include taxi aid video, cockpit door surveillance, smoke detection video (cargo and avionics bay), cabin video and airport navigation chart graphics.
	In compliance with airworthiness regulations, all mandatory flight instrument and aircraft system parameters, as well as cockpit conversations, are recorded by the flight data recording system (FDRS) and the cockpit voice recorder (CVR).
Navigation system	The navigation system comprises three key elements:
	• Navigation sources for aircraft position computation – these include the air data and inertial reference system (ADIRS). Other elements include navigation sensors such as multi-mode receivers (MMR), radio NAVAIDS and radio altimeters (RAs). The ADIRS is the aircraft navigation centre. It provides air data and inertial reference parameters to different aircraft systems (including the flight controls and the FMS) and to the CDS • A backup navigation system – the ISIS provides backup flight and navigation displays in the case of an ADIRS or related failure • Systems that provide assistance to the flight crew in various domains – for example, the SURVeillance (SURV) system alerts the flight crew to existing hazards, while the onboard airport navigation system (OANS) helps the flight crew find their way round the world's airports.
Oxygen system	The oxygen system is designed to supply oxygen to the flight crew, cabin crew and passengers, if necessary (for example, in case of depressurisation). It includes a fixed oxygen system in the cockpit and cabin and protective breathing equipment (PBE) for the cockpit, which comprises a hood that can be used below 25,000ft cabin altitude in the case of smoke, fire, noxious gas emissions or cabin depressurisation. The PBE protects the user's eyes and respiratory system for 15 minutes. The fixed cabin oxygen system provides oxygen in the cabin (for passengers and cabin crew), and in the crew rest compartments. It operates manually or automatically when the cabin altitude is higher than 13,800ft.

Avionics networks and IMA	All aircraft systems communicate with each other using two redundant avionics networks, instead of conventional wiring. These aircraft systems are monitored and controlled by conventional avionics, with computers that are assigned to specific systems, or IMA, with computers that can monitor and control several systems via several applications. All aircraft systems are connected to both avionics networks. The information that comes from the aircraft systems is transmitted to the avionics networks via various entry points, referred to as switches. These switches automatically manage the communication between the aircraft systems. Critical systems can always communicate with each other via conventional wiring to ensure that communication remains possible, if both avionics networks fail.
Onboard maintenance system (OMS)	The OMS is an integrated system providing support for aircraft servicing, line, scheduled and unscheduled maintenance, as well as aircraft configuration and reconfiguration monitoring. The OMS has three subsystems: • The central maintenance system (CMS) that identifies, centralises and memorises system failures • The aircraft condition monitoring system (ACMS) that provides operators with performance and trend information about aircraft systems and engines. The objective is to support scheduled and preventive maintenance, by monitoring the system parameters to improve the dispatch reliability • The DLCS that manages data loading and equipment configuration. The OMS is hosted on the NSS. It receives data from the avionics systems (through a secure communication interface) as well as data from the cabin systems. Maintenance data is transmitted to the operational ground centres and service providers during flight. The onboard maintenance terminal (OMT) is a portable multipurpose access terminal (PMAT) located in the cockpit between the third and fourth occupants' seats. It is the main terminal to interface with the OMS. During aircraft turnround or maintenance, the OMS can also be accessed by connecting a PMAT into one of the network ports installed on various aircraft locations.
Onboard information system (OIS)	The OIS is a set of electronic documentation and applications for flight, maintenance and cabin operations. For the flight crew, these applications replace the previously used paper documentation and charts. The main objective of the electronic documentation is to provide the flight crew with documentation in a format that enables easy access to the necessary information related to an operational need. OIS applications can be divided into: • Tools for flight operations support • Tools for cabin operations support • Tools for maintenance operations support • Services to the passengers, flight crew and cabin crew. The applications are hosted on three sub-networks or domains of the NSS: • The avionics domain – this includes the applications that exchange data with the aircraft avionics, including tools to support maintenance operations like the electronic logbook and CMS as well as electronic documentation that needs to be accessed by both flight and maintenance crew, including the minimum equipment list (MEL), configuration deviation list (CDL) and cabin crew operating manual (CCOM). It also includes a servicing tool dedicated to the refuelling operation • The flight operations domain – this includes the applications that support the flight crew on ground and in flight. These applications form part of the Airbus electronic flight bag (EFB) and include performance computation tools for take-off, in-flight and landing, a weight and balance (W&B) computation tool. Other documentation includes the flight crew operating manual (FCOM), aircraft flight manual (AFM), configuration deviation list (CDL), MEL, flight crew training manual (FCTM), as well as navigation and weather charts • The communication and cabin domain – this hosts the tools for cabin operations and maintenance, and services for passengers including e-mail and credit card banking.
Air traffic control (ATC) system	The ATC system enables data link communication between the aircraft and the ATC centres. The ATC system provides the flight crew and the avionics systems with communication, navigation and surveillance means. The data link communication between the aircraft and the ground network is made via the HF, VHF or SATCOM communication systems. The ATC application includes a notification function to establish a data link connection between the aircraft and the ATC centre by sending aircraft identity information such as the aircraft registration number and flight number. It also offers a datalink communication function enabling the flight crew to send requests and reports, and also read and answer messages.

CHAPTER 6

Cabin

OPPOSITE With unrivalled amounts of space, the A380 has enabled airlines to redefine the onboard experience for their passengers. *(Airbus)*

Introduction

For an airline's paying passengers, one of the most important aspects of their journey is undoubtedly onboard comfort and it is here that the A380 excels. Designed for the 21st-century aviation industry, the A380's unique size allows airlines to maximise their revenue potential through an optimised, segmented cabin. Airlines that successfully deploy the A380 on their high-yield, long-haul flights can enjoy greater market share, higher load factors and increased profitability.

The cabin is the quietest and most spacious in use today and for customer airlines, the super jumbo represents the ultimate in cabin customisation. Service offerings range from a comfortable 11-abreast economy section with 18in-wide seats, up to a private three-room suite for a luxurious first-class experience.

The A380's twin-aisle, twin-deck passenger cabin enhances the A380 travel experience and offers long-distance travellers a new level of space – in the form of wider seats and aisles – comfort and refinement, especially for those in the premium cabins.

The cabin occupies almost 70% of the overall aircraft's length and is typically configured with around 544 seats in four classes. In comparison with the Boeing 747-400, the A380 has 49% more floor area but only 35% more seats, thereby allowing more room for passengers to move about and for amenities to enhance the journey.

This chapter looks at the A380's innovative cabin design and some of the unique features on board that help to reduce traveller fatigue, with everything from fine dining to custom illumination systems and onboard relaxation areas. A closer look is also taken at how some of the world's leading airlines have customised and differentiated their aircraft in what is a very competitive market.

Cabin design

Soon after Airbus announced its intention to create a large double-deck airliner, bold new cabin concepts began emerging from airlines, cabin designers and Airbus itself. Many featured luxurious first-class products and business-class seats providing expansive space in which to work and relax. Among the more unlikely ideas were suggestions of gyms, casinos, beauty salons, restaurants, cinemas, a bowling alley and even swimming pools. The reality of airline operating economics soon put paid to anything too radical, but the A380 would soon set the standard for high-end premium accommodation with cabins featuring beds, sofas, showers and private areas for passengers.

BELOW A comparison between the Boeing 747 and Airbus A380 shows the additional space available on the world's largest commercial airliner.
(Roy Scorer)

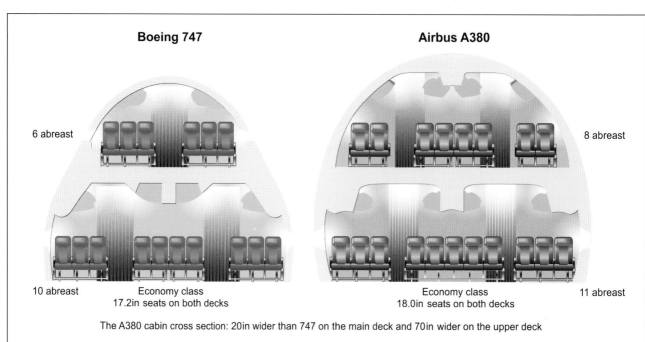

Boeing 747

Airbus A380

6 abreast

8 abreast

10 abreast

11 abreast

Economy class
17.2in seats on both decks

Economy class
18.0in seats on both decks

The A380 cabin cross section: 20in wider than 747 on the main deck and 70in wider on the upper deck

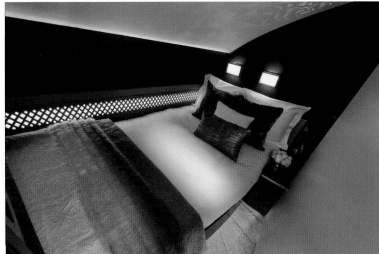

To facilitate the complex task of cabin design, Airbus supports the airline customer in a close and robust partnership providing knowledge and skills built up through years of customisation experience.

The optimum cabin arrangement is very specific to each airline and usually the result of several iterations. The type of classes with the required number of seats per class and spacing between seats are an essential input as a first step. Secondly, the airline defines cabin service needs such as galley space, the number of lavatories and required space for stowage.

THIS PAGE Airlines like Etihad have created a 'suite in the sky' for their premium customers. With a living room, separate bedroom and en-suite shower room, it is the only three-room suite on a commercial airline, designed for two people travelling together. The living room has a luxurious leather double-seat sofa and two dining tables. Passengers can enjoy an intimate meal and watch TV on a 32-inch flat screen through noise-cancelling headsets. The hallway leads to a bedroom with a 6-foot 10-inch double bed and passengers can freshen up in the en-suite shower room with full-height shower before landing. *(Airbus/Etihad)*

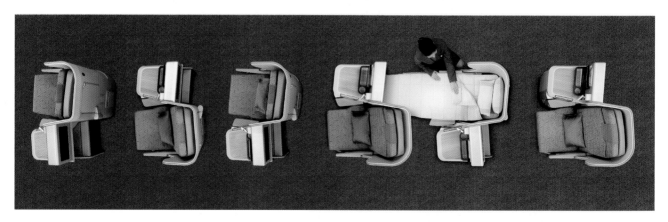

ABOVE Initial concepts are developed into physical full-size mock-ups and are tested with customers to help evaluate and narrow down options before an airline will commit to the final cabin design. *(Airbus)*

Design teams need to be conscious of what is technically feasible, the lead time involved as well as any relevant airworthiness regulations. The remaining fine-tuning is about balancing those key factors while meeting cost and weight targets.

Following the cabin arrangement, cabin systems are determined such as integrated IFE and/or connectivity to access the internet, live TV and phone services. Customers can customise lighting by choosing from a variety of colour and intensity options provided by cabin LED units (CLEDU), and can decide on visual projections such as logos and patterns.

To bring new technologies to the fore and excite passengers with imaginative design concepts, airlines tend to rely on renowned designers and specialised external design consultancies.

Agencies are typically tasked with defining and designing the passenger experience, which starts with customer research. This then translates into the cabin interior elements across all classes, such as galleys, lavatories and passenger destination zones, seating, catering and onboard service offer.

Initial concepts are then developed into physical full-size mock-ups and are tested with customers to help evaluate and narrow down the options. The design agency then typically develops the preferred concepts and builds a partial full-scale mock-up for development meetings and concept testing.

RIGHT The interior design in some A380s looks more like a hotel and less like an airliner. *(Airbus)*

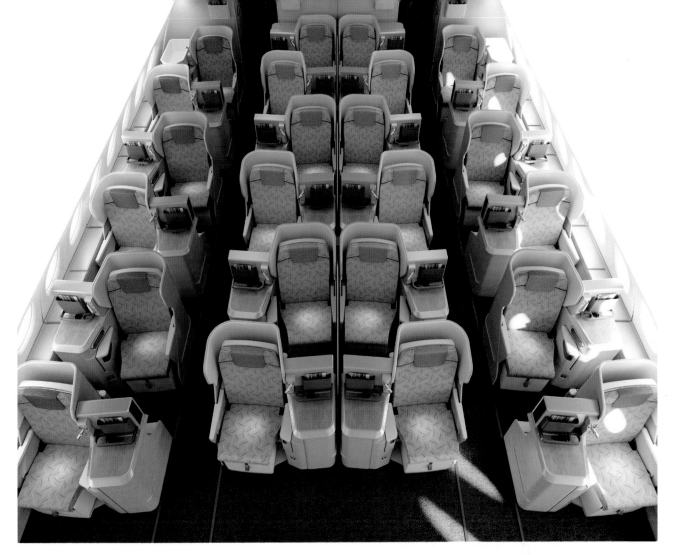

ABOVE Cabin design is a real art form, with the need to find a balance between stringent aviation safety regulations, weight requirements and the need to maximise commercial revenues. *(Airbus)*

The design team engages closely with Airbus and the chosen suppliers to understand the technical interfaces of the new concepts, supporting the airline through key design and technical decisions. As the designs become more defined, the mock-ups are updated to reflect the final product.

One such agency is PriestmanGoode, responsible for the A380 cabins of Lufthansa, Malaysia Airlines and Qatar Airways.

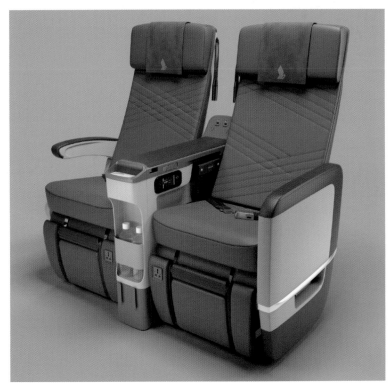

RIGHT Singapore Airlines' premium economy seat has several thoughtful touches showing the amount of consideration that's gone into its design. They are 19.5 inches wide and feature a greater degree of 'personal space' due to the wide armrest between the seats. *(Singapore Airlines)*

Director, Luke Hawes, said:

There are a number of difficulties in developing truly ground-breaking cabin designs. The first is purely in terms of research and development, the logistics of dealing with the stringent safety regulations and weight requirements of an aircraft. Beyond all of these practical issues though, it's important to remember that the A380 is a commercial aircraft, and space needs to be maximised to create revenue. So while gyms and cinemas sound appealing and are great as concepts, the reality of the airline industry is such that it's about seat count. But there might be one feature per airline, such as a bar, or a lounge that offers a good marketing story, which sits with the airline brand.

Cabin designers generally focus on trying to use the architecture of the aircraft to design in order to improve the passenger experience. As an example, the A380's main deck has almost straight sidewalls, creating a far more spacious feel for passengers.

The design team also works to ensure that the airline in question – often a national carrier – has its brand identity together with the country's culture and heritage reflected in the end product. 'When designing the Qatar A380 cabin, we modernised traditional Arabic patterns to create elegant bespoke features, creating a culturally sensitive cabin suited for the discerning global passenger,' said Hawes.

During their work on the Lufthansa A380 brief, the design team at PriestmanGoode were given the brief of 'creating a smoother transition from airport lounge to aircraft' for the airline's discerning business travellers. 'We developed a neutral palette in line with that of the first-class lounge at Frankfurt Airport, and designed seating to be more akin to lounge furniture than aircraft seating,' said Hawes.

Final assembly of the A380 takes place in Toulouse, with cabin fitting carried out in Hamburg.

Seating configurations

The dimensions of the A380 allow for both flexibility and creativity in cabin design and the A380 platform invites airlines to be more creative in the way they split up the area. That said, airlines need to strike a balance – they are ultimately in the business of transporting passengers where the key factor is the number of seats, and anything else they do to enhance the service competes with that. In the A380, more than in any other aircraft, the trade-off

BELOW In mid-2017 it emerged that Airbus were considering trimming its grand staircase to make room for 40-50 more seats. The wide staircase at the front of the plane would be replaced with a more compact design, while the slimmer spiral staircase at the back of the aircraft may also be modified. *(Airbus)*

DESIGNING THE QANTAS A380 CABIN

The opportunity to design a commercial aircraft cabin doesn't come along every day and when the opportunity was presented to Marc Newson it was a dream commission for the renowned Australian designer. 'Designing an aircraft interior offers a rare opportunity to create an artificial environment, which must shelter its occupants through the extremities of travelling across continents, weather systems and time zones at exceptionally high altitudes and speed,' says Marc. 'Designing an aircraft is like creating a mini-world – you're putting people in a confined environment and controlling how they'll feel there through the amount of oxygen that's pumped in, the humidity, and everything they touch and see. It all has an effect.' This was particularly important for Qantas, one of the world's longest-haul carriers.

Marc oversaw the design of all aspects of the interior. The brief included hundreds of different objects, including all of the accessories – trays, glasses, plates, cutlery, blankets, coat hooks, carpets, bathroom fittings, door knobs, reading lights, textiles and so on – as well as fixtures and the highly sophisticated and technically advanced aircraft seats. It was a significant brief as most of these objects had to be designed in four versions, one for each class: first, business, premium economy and economy.

The seating designed for the Qantas A380 across all of the classes incorporates advances in high-density cushioning materials, seating support frames, seat articulation mechanisms and fabrics. Space was gained through a reduction in bulk, providing considerable extra foot room and space for a larger, high-resolution digital screen.

With the designs of the Skybed, the A380 and the Sydney and Melbourne first-class lounges under his belt, Qantas appointed Marc their Creative Director in 2005, a position he held until 2014. Marc is now a Brand Ambassador for Qantas.

ABOVE Lufthansa's A380s are configured with 8 first, 78 business, 52 premium and 371 economy seats. *(Lufthansa)*

between using space for a seat or using it for an element that enhances the service around that seat, allows more variety.

The A380's upper and lower decks are connected by two stairways, fore and aft, and these are wide enough to accommodate two passengers side by side. This cabin arrangement allows multiple seating configurations and Airbus currently provide airline customers with 12 distinct A380 internal layouts. These include different combinations of interiors with overhead stowage compartments in a number of sizes, based on a modular system with common interface points.

The configuration of one deck can vary from that of the other, with different combinations of seating classes. Some industry analysts have suggested that implementing the extent of customisation available has raised costs, slowed production speeds and introduced complexity to the assembly process, but Airbus – and its customer airlines – would argue that these tailor-made solutions are vital to differentiating their product in a highly competitive market.

The maximum certified carrying capacity is 853 passengers in an all-economy class layout, and Airbus lists the 'typical' three-class layout as accommodating 525 passengers, with 10 first, 76 business and 439 economy-class seats.

The current trend is for operators to place the first, business and premium economy

ABOVE The sophisticated looking stairs leading from the main deck entrance to the upper deck on a British Airways A380. *(British Airways)*

Were an airline to operate an economy-only seating arrangement, the A380 could pack in more than 850 passengers (with 538 on the main deck and 315 on the upper deck of the aircraft) but the market dictates otherwise and more and more airlines are moving towards a four-class standard layout to accommodate the growing demand for a premium economy section. This has been driven by the large percentage of business travellers flying in economy.

The additional space afforded to airlines by the A380's design has been a real evolution in first- and business-class travel and allowed airlines to better address trends in premium-class accommodation. With some of the most unique offerings available in the sky, the A380 allows carriers to further differentiate their first-class cabin with a truly distinctive luxury product.

By restricting the number on board to 471 (barely 100 more than in an average 747), Singapore Airlines has chosen to give the extra space to passengers in every class. In economy, seats are an inch wider and, as a result of the seat design, passengers have more legroom; in business, seats are 34in wide; and in the 12 first-class cabins there's room for both an extra-wide seat (35in) and a separate 6ft 6in flat bed (a double if two of the cabins are put together).

More recently, consideration is being given to some of the A380's original cabins being reconfigured to accommodate an 11-seat row economy cabin, which has come about largely in response to market demand. The recession

classes on the upper deck, while configuring the main deck for an all-economy layout in a 10-abreast (3–4–3) or 11-abreast (3–5–3) seating layout, thereby keeping Airbus's standard 18in width between armrests. However, to maximise versatility, the main deck's seating in constant cross section can be configured in 4, 6, 7, 8, 10 and 11 abreast (9 also possible by adding a seat rail) and the upper deck's seating in 4, 6, 7 and 8 abreast.

BELOW Airbus has proposed the idea of an 11-seat economy cabin in a 3-5-3 configuration, however it has received a mixed response from airlines despite the additional revenue this configuration could generate. *(Airbus)*

– which began in 2008 – saw a drop in first-class and business seats and an increase in economy-class travellers. Among other causes is the reluctance of employers to pay for executives to travel in premium seats.

Evacuation

The A380's flexibility means that many cabin configurations can be installed, although they must all strictly respect airworthiness authorities' requirements and safety measures. Airbus ensures that the customised cabin meets these criteria. Passengers must be uniformly distributed in each zone in order to comply with the evacuation plan. Currently the maximum number of passengers in an A380 is 853 as agreed with the airworthiness authorities. To comply with the emergency evacuation requirements, all passengers and crew must be able to leave the cabin within 90 seconds. Tests on the A380 were performed in 78 seconds, well within the prescribed limit.

Cabin amenities

The Airbus A380 is indeed in a league of its own when it comes to passenger amenities and comfort. The sheer size of the aircraft has enabled airlines to give passengers more space in their seats and the opportunity to be creative with amenities, given the room they have to work with.

On board, use is made of some of the latest technologies including advanced lighting systems and new standards of in-flight entertainment. Cabin air is recycled every two minutes to keep the atmosphere fresh, while 220 large cabin windows provide natural light. Four high-level air outlets – as opposed to the industry standard of two – keep customers refreshed during all phases of flight. Coupled with its optimal cabin height, these key advantages deliver more personal space all over the aircraft whether that is for storage, better headroom or even wider stairs creating a welcoming environment. Some of the key amenities and features include:

■ 50% less cabin noise, 50% more cabin area and volume, bigger overhead bins, and

ABOVE The A380 was thoroughly tested to ensure it could comply with the strict emergency evacuation requirements. *(Airbus)*

BELOW As with any commercial airliner, the evacuation procedures for the A380 are provided on a safety leaflet for passengers. *(Author)*

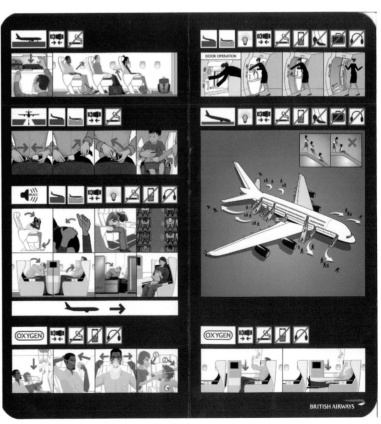

60cm of extra headroom compared to the Boeing 747-400
■ The widest main deck cabin and the first wide-body upper deck
■ Total cabin surface area of some 550m²
■ Large windows measuring 38cm × 28cm
■ 18in-wide economy-class seats at 11 abreast compared to 17in on the 747 at 10 abreast

■ Cabin mood lighting which can be altered to create an ambience simulating daylight, night or intermediate levels. The lighting is not only a key element in the feeling of comfort for passengers, but also plays a role in synchronising the body clock
■ The lowest number of passengers per temperature control zone of any aircraft flying today
■ The cabin is split into 15 different temperature control zones, the temperature in each can be varied between 18 and 30°C. Designed to reduce traveller fatigue, the cabin has higher pressurisation than previous generations of aircraft
■ The A380 is equipped with three external mini-cameras located at the front, below and at the rear of the plane and the feed from these cameras is transmitted live throughout the flight
■ For the cabin crews, life is made easier too, courtesy of a separate network known as the cabin intercommunication and data

WIRING WOES

Several airlines, particularly those who were early adopters of the A380, elected to load their aircraft on order with an array of amenities to lure high-spending travellers for whom comfort was more important than price. Many of these proposed features required more complex wiring that had to be added to existing harnesses used to carry data and provide the juice for everything from avionics to in-flight entertainment.

These requirements caused some setbacks and delays in early production for Airbus as the basic wiring setup was being modified for each customer, depending on the selected amenities. Despite importing engineers and technicians from its factory in Hamburg in an attempt to keep production on schedule, wiring difficulties would delay deliveries by anything from six months to a year.

RIGHT **Complex wiring was needed to power and operate the array of amenities installed in the first A380s, which resulted in unexpected setbacks and delays in early production.** *(Author)*

system, which manages services including cabin communications, lighting, doors and passenger calls. Up to 10 touchscreen flight attendant panels can be installed across the aircraft to aid the crew.

Airlines increasingly view aircraft as a premium product – a flagship on which to introduce new amenities and service concepts that give them an advantage over the competition – and innovative new ideas to enhance the passenger experience are sure to be revealed.

In-flight entertainment

In the fiercely contested premium air travel segment, in-flight entertainment ranks alongside seat comfort as the key differentiator and airlines have been compelled to make significant investments in ground-breaking systems. Today's in-flight entertainment systems on the A380 provide passengers with an astonishing array of films, TV programmes, interactive games, audio CDs and even language lessons.

The systems tend to be based on a high-speed fibre-optic Ethernet backbone, reducing both wiring and weight. Content is contained on servers with capacity of 10 terabytes, while video display units in the seat backs process data locally. With increased bandwidth to each seat, quality, choice and fluidity for passengers has reached a new level.

The Singapore Airlines system, for example, provides audio and video on demand in all three seating classes and features 100 movies, 150 TV programmes, 22 broadcast radio channels, 710 music CDs and multiplayer games. Increased levels of redundancy have also been built into the system to ensure that any failures are limited to a minimum number of seats.

British Airways' A380s are fitted with the latest version of the airline's Thales in-flight entertainment system with more than 1,600 hours of programming, 550 audio albums and 225 radio shows. The system also includes the 3D Interactive GeoFusion flight map with high-resolution graphics of the world's major cities.

AIR FRANCE DIGITAL GALLERY

On board its Airbus A380s, Air France is the first airline to offer an in-flight gallery concept, thanks to its partnerships with major museums worldwide and other artistic institutions. This type of open-plan area is the most spacious offered by any airline. Air France offers its La Première and business customers the opportunity each month to discover, in the gallery located on the upper deck of the aircraft, artistic exhibitions presented in a video format on three 38cm screens. Since its launch, the Air France gallery has presented works of international artists from prestigious museums and art institutes such as the Musée du Louvre, the Palazzo Grassi in Venice and the Museum of Modern Art (MoMA) in New York.

ABOVE In the fiercely contested premium air travel segment, in-flight entertainment ranks alongside seat comfort as the key differentiator and airlines have been compelled to make significant investments in ground-breaking systems. (Airbus)

ABOVE LEFT Even in the economy cabins, today's in-flight entertainment systems on the A380 provide passengers with an astonishing array of digital content. (Singapore Airlines

Airline examples

The A380's double-deck configuration and built-in flexibility allows airlines to differentiate their products and develop solutions for specific market mixes. Here's how some of the different airlines have created their cabins:

In-service A380 cabin layouts
13 operators using 16 different configurations

	First	Business	Premium economy	Economy	Total seats	A380s in service
	12	86	36	245	**379**	8
	12	60	36	333	**441**	11
	14	76	–	401	**491**	32
	14	76	–	429	**519**	53
	–	58	–	557	**615**	8
	14	64	35	371	**484**	12
	9	80	38	389	**516**	10
	8	78	52	371	**509**	14
	12	94	–	301	**407**	10
	8	70	–	428	**506**	5
	8	66	–	420	**494**	6
	12	60	–	435	**507**	6
	14	97	55	303	**469**	12
	12	66	–	417	**495**	6
	8	48	–	461	**517**	7
	11	70	–	417	**498**	8

RIGHT The current 13 operators of the A380 use 16 different cabin configurations – Singapore Airlines and Emirates are the only two with varying options within their respective fleets.

(Author)

Singapore Airlines

Airbus and Singapore Airlines started the A380 cabin design process in the late 1990s. The resulting Singapore Airlines Suites, located on the aircraft's main deck, were conceived by French yacht designer Jean-Jacques Coste and manufactured by Tokyo-based Jamco Corp. and Sicma Aero Seat of Issoudun, France, according to the airline. They contain a nearly metre-wide (39in) fully adjustable seat, a separate full-size bed with plush mattress and a 23in LCD display for in-flight entertainment.

The 60 passengers in business class, located on the upper deck, have 34in-wide seats that can be converted into fully flat beds. The only airline operating the A380 which allows you to convert two seats into a double bed is Singapore's Suites Class.

(Rolando Ugolini)

British Airways

British Airways A380s are configured with a total of 469 seats split across the airline's familiar cabins: first (14 suites), Club World (97 business class), World Traveller Plus (55 premium economy) and World Traveller (303 economy seats).

BA effectively treats the A380 as if it's one aircraft loaded on top of another. Business and economy are split with some seats on both levels, with first class at the front of the main deck, and business class split, with 44 seats in a 2–4–2 configuration on the main deck, and 53 seats in a 2–3–2 configuration on the upper deck. The airline's intention, it seems, is to keep the premium travellers closer to the front of the aeroplane to make it quicker and easier for them to get on and off.

(Rolando Ugolini)

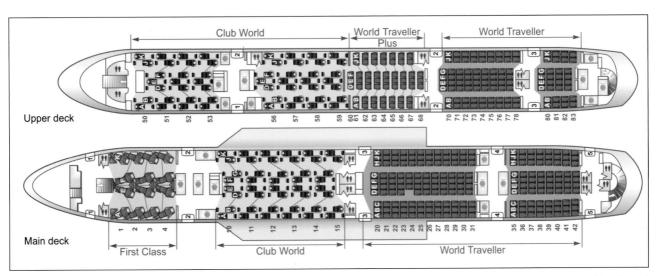

(Roy Scorer)

Premium economy is in a 2–3–2 configuration upstairs, but economy is also split – downstairs there are 199 seats in a 3–4–3 configuration while upstairs there are 104 seats in a 2–4–2 setup. This arrangement provides a variety of seating options for families of different sizes.

The ergonomic seats in the suites convert into fully flat beds, 6ft 6in in length and customers are offered British Airways' signature Turndown Service during which cabin crew make up beds using a crisp white mattress, duvet, pillow and nightwear. During the flight passengers enjoy entertainment on a 15.4in personal in-flight entertainment touchscreen with noise-cancelling headphones.

(All drawings on this spread Rolando Ugolini)

Qantas

Qantas has opted to put the best and the worst on one level, and those in between on the other: first class and economy are on the main (lower) deck, while business and premium economy share the upper deck.

Air France

The 516 passengers on board Air France's A380 enjoy more comfort and space, whichever cabin they are travelling in: La Première on the upper deck (9 seats), the business cabin (80 seats) and Premium Voyageur (38 seats) on the upper deck and the Voyageur Economy cabin, located on both decks (389 seats including 46 on the upper deck).

On board, Air France has designed everything so that passengers enjoy a quiet and particularly soothing cabin with noise levels which are 5dB lower than industry standards.

The colour schemes and lighting have been chosen to make the atmosphere as relaxed as possible. The gallery area, the six bars located in all cabins and the stairs connecting the two decks are geared towards relaxation and conviviality.

Lufthansa

The flagship German carrier doesn't have a premium economy class and uses the full lower deck for economy seating. First class is upstairs and business class is right behind it. At Frankfurt Airport, Lufthansa has a boarding lounge area upstairs, allowing premium passengers to sit in a lounge environment and then directly board the upper deck of the aircraft. It's a more traditional boarding process down below for those in the cheaper seats.

Emirates

There are good reasons to have first class upstairs, as shown by Emirates. The front of the upper deck has a large stairway, which leaves some rather awkward spaces on either side. Making the most of this, Emirates created mega-bathrooms with showers for first-class passengers. Naturally, that led the airline to put first class up top. Business is behind first, and economy on the lower deck in a similar configuration to that of Lufthansa.

The 'shower spas' were first introduced in 2008 and allow each first-class passenger five minutes of hot water, drawing on 2.5 tonnes of water. These are manned by full-time shower attendants on long-haul flights, who are exclusively there to clean the shower suites and bathrooms.

In late 2016 Emirates began taking delivery of its new-generation Airbus A380 aircraft. In addition to its iconic onboard lounge and first-class shower spa, the new-generation Emirates A380 – 58 of which are on order – has several innovative features, including a new seating configuration. The crew rest area has been relocated, creating space for 25 additional economy-class seats, making a total of 426 seats on the lower deck. First- and business-class seats remain at 14 and 76 respectively.

Among the features is an elegant new design in the business-class cabin with a higher ceiling to create a more spacious and luxurious feel for customers. Overhead cabin lockers are concentrated in the middle aisles and are almost 30% larger in volume.

Qatar Airways

The gulf state's A380s feature a tri-class configuration of seating in first, business and economy class over the two decks.

The 1–2–1 configuration ensures that every seat business class is an aisle seat. Other amenities include onboard Wi-Fi and fully lie-flat seats that come with designer cotton sleeper suits and slippers.

Higher ceilings on the main deck and a configuration that uses fewer seats, contributes to a feeling of spaciousness. The airline's in-flight entertainment system offers passengers a choice of some 3,000 movies, TV box sets, music and games.

Etihad Airways

Etihad's new A380 aircraft are probably best known for their VIP cabins called 'The Residence', a private three-room suite that features a living room, bedroom and private bathroom with shower. Best of all, there's also a Savoy-trained butler who is exclusively responsible for taking care of you.

Chapter 7

Airport compatibility

OPPOSITE A Qantas A380 on stand at Heathrow Airport in London after arriving from Sydney. *(Waldo van der Waal)*

Introduction

With a wingspan of 79.5m and a maximum take-off weight of 545,000kg, the arrival of the A380 was something of a double-edged sword for many airports. Those experiencing capacity problems would see passenger throughput increased without any additional aircraft movements, but on the flipside, the increased scale of the A380 would present them a series of infrastructure challenges.

Well before the launch of the super jumbo, Airbus recognised that besides the requirement to use existing ground handling equipment, the A380 also needed to fit into today's airport infrastructure with minimal changes.

Some newer airports were well placed to deal with the aircraft, while older ones had to make a variety of upgrades that included the need for wider and longer runways, wider taxiways, upgrades to baggage handling systems, dual passenger boarding bridges, increased time for passenger boarding and space for passenger amenities, to mention just a few examples.

Airports where large-scale infrastructure changes were considered economical included the large continental gateways, and those airports whose home-carriers had ordered the A380 aircraft, for example: Heathrow, Paris Charles de Gaulle, Frankfurt, New York, Los Angeles, Singapore, Hong Kong, Sydney and Dubai.

In a few cases, buildings even had to be

LEFT **Air traffic controllers in the Heathrow tower get a good view of this A380 as it heads to the departure runway.** *(Waldo van der Waal)*

relocated to provide sufficient wingtip clearance, while at some airports, runway lighting and signage was moved to avoid damage from jet blast during take-off. As the A380's jet blast contours exceed those of other wide-body aircraft, airports also had to give due consideration to ensuring safe working and operating conditions. Air traffic controllers were also required to work to new guidelines, with increased lateral separation between an A380 and other aircraft.

Fortunately, Airbus understood these challenges early on and right from the initial stages of the A380's design, the manufacturer involved all stakeholders – including regulatory authorities, ground equipment manufacturers, ground handlers, airport authorities and airlines – to ensure the aircraft was optimised for smooth, safe and efficient airport operations. In support of this, an A380 test aircraft participated in an extensive campaign of airport compatibility testing to verify the modifications already made at a number of airports around the world.

Despite the initial challenges, A380s are now compatible for scheduled destinations and alternate operations at more than 140 airports, with more than 400 compatible destination and alternate airports expected in the near future.

Regulatory considerations

Like any manufacturer, Airbus had to be sure their aircraft could work within the aviation sector's regulatory framework, in particular those standards and practices advised by the International Civil Aviation Organization (ICAO).

The ICAO works with 191 member states and industry groups to reach consensus on international civil aviation standards in support of a safe, efficient, secure, economically sustainable and environmentally responsible civil aviation sector. Their policies enable more than 100,000 daily flights in aviation's global network to operate safely and reliably in every region of the world.

In addition to working closely with the ICAO, Airbus actively sought and acted upon the comments of airport operators and airlines, using these inputs to optimise the aircraft for airport compatibility.

In many respects, the A380 was designed to minimise the need for airports to upgrade infrastructure and a pan-European group of civil aviation authorities and airport operators, known as the A380 Airport Compatibility Group (AACG), developed a set of specific operational recommendations to permit A380 operations at

ABOVE Engineers scale new heights on this Qantas A380 pre-flight inspection at Heathrow. *(Waldo van der Waal)*

existing airports with minimal changes.

This process proved very beneficial and assisted several airports in keeping projected upgrade expenditure at lower levels than expected. Careful compromises enabled airports to be certificated for A380 operations while minimising capital expenditure and operational disruption, with the end goal being to have a footprint that was not significantly larger than that of the 747.

Some of the operational recommendations allowed for A380 movements at airports classified by ICAO as Code E facilities (which are designed for smaller wide-body aircraft such

ICAO AERODROME REFERENCE CODES

Code letter	Wingspan	Outer main gear wheelspan	Typical aeroplane
A	Up to but not including 15m	Up to but not including 4.5m	Piper PA-31/Cessna 404
B	15m up to but not including 24m	4.5m up to but not including 6m	Bombardier Regional Jet CRJ-200
C	24m up to but not including 36m	6m up to but not including 9m	Boeing 737/Airbus A320
D	36m up to but not including 52m	9m up to but not including 14m	Boeing 767/Airbus A310
E	52m up to but not including 65m	9m up to but not including 14m	Boeing 777/787 A330
F	65m up to but not including 80m	14m up to but not including 16m	Boeing 747-8/Airbus A380

The reference codes are intended to provide a simple method for interrelating the numerous specifications concerning the characteristics of aerodromes in order to provide a series of facilities (such as the runways and stands) that are suitable for the aircraft intended to operate at the aerodrome or airport. The code is not intended to be used for determining runway length or pavement strength requirements.

as the A330 and A350 XWB) with little or no changes to the existing airport infrastructure.

At those airports where upgrades were required, changes varied from airport to airport and included: runway and taxiway pavement and/or shoulders, jet blast pads, taxiway bridges, ground vehicle tunnels, signs, lights, pavement markings, aircraft rescue and firefighting equipment, gates, fuel pits, airbridges, passenger lounges, drainage, utilities and aircraft maintenance hangars.

Upgrading aircraft rescue and firefighting equipment was a key issue as emergency services at airports had to ensure they could access the upper deck of the A380 to fight a fire and/or evacuate passengers. Airports also had to make provision to deal with the post-evacuation safety of an unprecedented number of evacuees.

Benefits for airports

Just as larger aircraft have done throughout history, the arrival of the A380 has generated a wide range of benefits for airports – passenger growth, increased revenue and sustainable growth. Of particular interest to airports is the aircraft's extra capacity as well as its environmental characteristics, but the range of benefits extends still further:

■ **More passengers per stand and slot** – the A380 provides the highest level of infrastructure efficiency of any wide-body

ABOVE Extensive airport trials were conducted to ensure the A380 could successfully enter service. (Waldo van der Waal)

LEFT Airports had to invest in new, taller fire-fighting equipment, such as this vehicle at Heathrow, to enable emergency services to reach the A380's upper deck.
(Waldo van der Waal)

aircraft and growth for airports with limited extra flights. In fact, without A380s replacing smaller aircraft on many routes, some airports would have no choice but to build more gates, more parking spaces and eventually additional runways in order to provide room for ever higher frequencies. Airports benefit as extra passengers can be served at key hubs during high-value peak times.

■ **Higher maximum take-off weight** – offering higher aeronautical revenue charged to airlines associated with each A380 movement.

■ **Higher passenger throughput** – resulting in higher non-aeronautical revenues such as passenger charges and duty-free spend.

■ **Network effect** – the aircraft supports hub airports and increased regional traffic, Dubai Airport (DXB) – together with Emirates – being a great example of this phenomenon.

■ **Lowest overall environmental impact**

– compared to the Boeing 747, the A380 carries 60% more passengers, generates half the noise and 40% less CO_2 emissions per passenger. In fact, the aircraft offers the lowest fuel-burn per seat of any large aircraft. This is a significant factor at congested airports such as London Heathrow where the demand for an additional runway has been a controversial topic of debate for many years and at last appears to have been given the go-ahead.

■ **Outstanding performance** – the A380 offers better take-off and climb performance, lower approach speeds and automated as well as customised noise abatement departure procedures – providing noise reduction for noise-sensitive areas in close proximity to the departure end of the runway. At airports like Heathrow, neighbours have publicly praised the A380's remarkable noise performance.

■ **Points of difference** – passengers are drawn to the twin-deck aircraft and features such as being able to board the aircraft directly from the lounge make for a seamless transition from ground to air.

Take-off and landing separation

Having an A380 take off or land at an airport presented some new challenges to ATC teams. The aircraft's size means the vortices generated are more substantial than for other aircraft in the 'Heavy' wake turbulence category.

These vortices form behind an aircraft as it passes through the air, creating a hazardous area in its wake – even more so one the size of an A380 – in the take-off or landing phases of flight. For air traffic controllers, looking after multiple inbound and outbound aircraft, all operating at low speed and low height, specific consideration had to be given to the separation between aircraft to minimise any potential dangers.

In 2005, the ICAO recommended that the giant aircraft's wake vortex characteristics demanded special treatment and implemented a provisional set of separation requirements for the aircraft during approach, take-off and cruise. The news came as a potentially disastrous setback to Airbus and threatened to wipe out any capacity gain the A380 could offer busy airports like London Heathrow, by reducing the

BELOW A China Southern A380 touches down – the giant aircraft would present some new challenges to air traffic controllers. *(Airbus)*

number of landings per hour that the airport could handle. Airbus set about protesting the recommendations and immediately commenced further testing ahead of the aircraft's entry into service. The tests included flying the A380 and 747 using complex technology to detect, measure and visualise wake turbulence.

Following further study, the initial blanket 10nm separation for aircraft trailing an A380 during approach, was reduced to 6nm, 8nm and 10nm respectively for Heavy, Medium, and Light ICAO aircraft categories. Though not identical to the separation minima for the Boeing 747, the revised ICAO guidance helped Airbus move closer to its goal.

On departure behind an A380, Heavy aircraft are required to wait two minutes, and Medium/Light aircraft three minutes. ICAO also recommended that pilots append the term 'Super' to the aircraft's callsign when initiating communication with ATC, to distinguish the A380 from 'Heavy' aircraft such as the Boeing 747.

In mid-2008, revised approach separations of 6nm for Heavy, 7nm for Medium and 8nm for Light aircraft were introduced.

Runways and taxiways

It's easy to imagine that an aircraft with the enormous bulk of the A380 would have a detrimental effect on the runways it was landing on, but extensive testing by Airbus demonstrated that the weight of the plane would not cause unnecessary stress and very few would need reinforcing.

A key factor in this was the A380's rather remarkable 20-wheel main landing gear. As the A380 uses more landing wheels than other large jets, each wheel actually transmits less weight to the runway than some other aircraft, making it very friendly to the airport pavement.

Airbus measured pavement loads using a 540-tonne ballasted test rig, designed to replicate the aircraft's landing gear. Using a section of pavement at Airbus's facilities that had been embedded with load sensors, testing determined that the pavement of most runways would not need to be reinforced despite the aircraft's higher weight.

Generally speaking, most major runways are long enough for the aircraft's take-off and landing procedures, though some were not quite wide enough (the A380's engines would hang over the edges slightly).

Initially, ICAO's Code F recommendations – which apply to airports handling aircraft with wingspans between 65m and 80m and an outer main gear wheelspan of between 14m and 16m – were enforced. For the A380, which has a wingspan of 79.8m – just below the Code F limit – a runway width of 60m was the prescribed code, whereas the baseline for airports that were built to cater for the 747 is the Code E specification of 45m.

Then, in a significant win for Airbus in July 2007, the group received regulatory approval for the A380 to be operated on standard-width runways. ICAO still recommends the new aircraft be provided with 60m-wide runways, and some airports at which many A380 movements take place have carried out widening work in order to be compliant. At

ABOVE In the case of the A380, studies have shown the impact on airfield pavements of additional operations will fare between modest and non-existent.
(Waldo van der Waal)

ABOVE Singapore Airlines' A380s are a regular sight at Heathrow. The airline also flies the aircraft to 15 other international destinations. (Author)

some airports, runway lighting and signage needed changes to provide clearance to the wings and avoid blast damage from the engines – easier to appreciate when one considers the A380's outboard engines are more than 25m from the centreline of the aircraft, compared to 21m for the Boeing 747.

Stand size and equipment

It is interesting to note that back in the late 1990s, when aircraft manufacturers were planning to introduce larger planes than the Boeing 747, ICAO reached consensus with manufacturers, airports and its member agencies on a number of key dimensions – those of arrival and departure gates, widths of runways and taxiways, spacing between parallel runways and strength of bridges that larger aircraft would need to traverse.

Perhaps the most significant measurement that was agreed was that of the stand size, known simply as the '80-metre box'. This effectively meant that airport gates could

RIGHT The A380's outboard engines are more than 25m from the centreline of the aircraft, compared to 21m for the Boeing 747. (Airbus)

RIGHT A Qantas A380 sits on the apron at
Heathrow – the airline provides connecting flights
from both Sydney and Melbourne via Dubai.
(Author)

accommodate aircraft up to 80m or 262.5ft
wingspan and length. So significant was this
number that it came to dominate the aircraft's
design.

The A380's wingspan, at 79.8m, just
makes it into the box, leaving less than 6in
on either side. Yet despite this constraint,
the A380 is highly compatible with existing
airport infrastructure, allowing for smooth
airline operations and differentiated services for
passengers. It is designed to reduce time at the
gate during critical stages for airlines: boarding
and deboarding passengers and resupplying
the galley for the next flight.

The ground servicing equipment needed for
the A380 has been in service since the aircraft
began commercial flights and is compatible with
other wide-body aircraft. By and large, airports
need no new equipment to deal with the A380
during the all-important turnround process, with
existing wide-body ground equipment being
put into action on the stand. That said, airports
soon realised the value of employing an upper
deck catering vehicle which significantly reduces
the catering critical path to 90 minutes, less
than that required for a Boeing 747.

Another contributor to improved turnround
times is use of secondary airbridges, allowing
passengers to simultaneously board both
levels of the aircraft. The A380's superior
cabin architecture means upper airbridges are
not mandatory and several airports currently
operate without them.

A standard 50-tonne tow tractor for
pushback is also considered sufficient for
handling the A380 in most conditions. In
adverse traction conditions a 70-tonne tractor
may be required.

Passenger boarding

While airlines welcome the additional
revenue from the increased passenger
numbers carried on an A380, these seats need
to be emptied and then filled in an efficient

fashion to minimise the time that the aircraft
spends on the ground. Two levels of passenger
seating, combined with several entry points to
the plane, provide both an unparalleled capacity
and previously unseen potential for fast loading.

Furthermore, the ability to board passengers
simultaneously on both the upper and main
deck provides airlines (and airports) with a
real point of differentiation. For example, while
economy-class passengers board the main
deck, airlines can offer a customised service to
their premium passengers on the upper deck by

BELOW Airports soon
realised the value of
employing an upper
deck catering vehicle,
which significantly
reduces the catering
critical path to 90
minutes. (Author)

RIGHT BA A380 with
registration XLEB on
stand at Heathrow
Terminal 5 with main
and upper airbridges
in operation. (Author)

was the preferred option. Airbus insists two bridges will be adequate, and the option of a third bridge is up to the airlines and airports.

Airports serving carriers with a high proportion of A380 transfer traffic (like Singapore and Dubai) have tended to opt for three bridges because passenger throughput is the key priority. Airbus estimates that when using two airbridges the boarding time is 45 minutes and when using an extra bridge to the upper deck it is reduced to 34 minutes.

Diversion airports

Before taking their aircraft to operational service, an airline's team of flight operations engineers spent time working on flight progress charts. These maps show the air routes and diversion (alternate) airports to determine which airfield a flight crew could divert to in the event of an emergency.

Such diversions could be due either to the unavailability of the destination airport (because of weather or operational issues) or because of an in-flight emergency. It is in the interest of in-flight safety to have a reasonable number of alternate airports and runways available in addition to the scheduled ones.

These are ranked from 'primary preferred' down to 'emergency only'. Development of flight progress charts for the A380 is an interesting challenge as there are fewer airports that can accept the aircraft given its size.

Airports that are regularly used for A380 operations must meet defined standards but as occurrences of flight diversions are relatively low and many alternate airports will see only a few diversions a year or, in the case of emergency alternates, may never see one, it is reasonable to expect these airports to maintain the level of operational safety by use of alternative measures, operational procedures and operating restrictions.

enabling them to board directly from the airport lounge – a seamless transition from the ground to the air.

A key consideration for all A380 airports is whether to add a third airbridge to smooth the flow of passengers during turnround. Airbus initially suggested two bridges to doors on the main deck. Talks with airlines soon led the manufacturer to realise that an airbridge to the upper deck (as well as one to the main deck)

BELOW The ability
to board passengers
simultaneously on
both the upper and
main deck provides
airlines (and airports)
with a real point of
differentiation. (Author)

Maintenance, repair and overhaul (MRO)

MRO is the blanket term for organisations providing all the services relating to assuring aircraft safety and airworthiness, including the preparation and planning of scheduled maintenance programmes to real-time health monitoring and troubleshooting and structural repair, as well as the management of technical data and documentation.

Given its size and the multitude of evolutionary technologies employed on the aircraft, the A380 presents some interesting challenges from an MRO perspective. For example, German flag carrier Lufthansa recognised early that the largest long-haul aircraft ever built demanded some fairly significant investments in infrastructure, equipment and training. In fact their technical arm, Lufthansa Technik, was involved along with other A380 customers early on in the A380's development, contributing to the development of maintenance schedules for the A380.

The next step following the completion of their dedicated A380 hangar was the acquisition of all necessary tools and equipment for servicing the new aircraft, an example of which were tripod jacks to lift the aircraft for landing gear maintenance and special torque wrenches to remove and install the engine mounts.

A further need for upgrades in ground support equipment was also identified. One example was the construction of a new tail dock to provide easy access to the A380's systems in this area, including the APU, flight control actuators, elevator, stabiliser and the tailfin itself. Scaffolding and maintenance platforms need to be more than 24m tall, much

higher than on any other aircraft currently in service. Lufthansa also invested in new tow equipment to move the A380 between the terminal and the maintenance area. The AST-1X tow tractor, with its 1,300hp engine and six driven wheels, is capable of towing the Airbus A380 (at 560 tonnes) at up to 20mph.

Emirates' MRO facilities currently comprise 11 A380-sized hangars, a separate paint facility and an engine overhaul shop, designed to

ABOVE In 2015, China Southern transported more than 110 million passengers, surpassing all other carriers in Asia. *(Airbus)*

LEFT An Etihad Airways A380 undergoes a routine maintenance check in Abu Dhabi. *(Airbus)*

MAINTENANCE, REPAIR AND OVERHAUL

With a view to ensuring efficient MRO operations during the lifespan of the A380, customer airlines like Lufthansa made a significant contribution early on during the development of the aircraft. MRO service providers expect an aircraft to be designed in such a way that work can be carried out quickly, easily, ergonomically and with the smallest possible number of special tools. Ultimately, clear solutions were found that maximise both the operational efficiency as well as the technical reliability without compromising safety and paved the way for a smooth entry in service. *(Lufthansa)*

TYPICAL MAINTENANCE CHECKS FOR ANY AIRCRAFT TYPE

■ **A-check** – performed approximately every 500–1,200 flight hours. The check requires about 50–70 man hours and the aircraft is usually on the ground for a minimum of 10 hours (overnight).

■ **B-check** – this is rarely used nowadays, but originally referred to a block check performed between an A-check and a C-check. B-check tasks are today typically consolidated in A-check packages.

■ **C-check** – performed approximately at 18–36 months or a specified number of aircraft flight hours. This maintenance check is more extensive than a B-check (or multiple A-check) requiring a more detailed inspection of aircraft system functions. The A380 C-check is expected to increase from 24 months to 36 months in early 2018.

■ **D-check** – this happens every 6 or 12 years, with the latter period typically requiring inspection of pretty much the entire aircraft. The aircraft is not actually taken apart although a number of components will be removed, particularly from within the cabin, to allow inspection of the structure. Although cabin furnishings will be replaced or refurbished at this check, only a small number of aircraft components need to be overhauled; most will simply be inspected and reinstalled.

refurbish some 300 engines each year. More significant repairs are carried out by the original equipment manufacturers (OEM) but Emirates is rapidly moving to a self-sufficient model by expanding its in-house engine capabilities.

The A380 has a flexible maintenance programme with no defined block checks. The scheduled tasks are defined at fixed intervals with the objective to check whether there is degradation or failure. There is condition-based maintenance driven by sensors that highlight when maintenance is necessary. The approach allows airline operators to optimise maintenance planning to match their utilisation and operational priorities. That said, typical inspection intervals are as follows:

- A Check – 750 to 1,000 flying hours
- C Check – 24 to 36 months
- Intermediate layover – six years (light structural maintenance addressing corrosion and zonal inspections)
- Structures maintenance – 12 years
- Landing gear overhaul – 12 years

A heavy maintenance check on the world's largest passenger plane is no small task and can typically take around 50–55 days to complete. During a recent Emirates A380 heavy maintenance check, more than 1,600 parts were removed from the cabin, overhauled, and put back into place. Each of the four engines were also removed, inspected and overhauled.

LUFTHANSA TECHNIK

When Lufthansa took delivery of their first A380 in May 2010, a considerable amount of preparatory work had been carried out in advance. First was the preparation of Lufthansa Technik's facilities, comprised of two new hangars (in Beijing and Frankfurt). The latter was completed in December 2007 and measures 180m × 140m; its height of 45m provides enough space to easily accommodate two A380s and sufficient overhead clearance to lift the aircraft to any height required for maintenance.

Neighbouring the new hangar, Lufthansa Technik Logistik has set up a new spare parts pool with more than 8,500m^2 of space and more than 70,000 different parts in its inventory, ranging from the smallest screws to the largest components.

To maintain and support the A380's engine, Lufthansa's Engine Overhaul Services facility – a joint venture with the engine's manufacturer Rolls-Royce – represents one of the world's most advanced and best-equipped engine shops worldwide. And as for avionics, the A380 is the first plane that features an onboard maintenance terminal to control and monitor its integrated modular avionics system via a single interface, thus reducing costs, saving time and ensuring quality.

The facility also provides three aircraft parking positions, two of them suitable for engine run-up tests. For safety reasons and to prevent the jet wash from damaging the surroundings during these tests, a completely new blast fence had to be set up. With its own concrete foundation, the fence, 80m in length and 12m high, is now capable of deflecting even the strongest jet wash of the A380's four engines, which are mounted wider than on any other commercial airliner.

LEFT Up close and personal with a Lufthansa A380. (Lufthansa)

ABOVE Health monitoring is a form of system diagnosis, the goal of which is to detect system failure and identify which component is responsible for it. The diagnosis is based on information derived from signals originating from built-in sensors and detectors. *(Author)*

AiRTHM

Airbus Real Time Health Monitoring (AiRTHM) is an advanced service through which A380 (and A350) operators receive guidance on optimised maintenance and real-time troubleshooting actions. As part of this effort, a dedicated 24/7 team takes advantage of the uplink technology to further investigate and anticipate warnings/fault consequences. This allows real-time remote access to aircraft data parameters via the ACARS digital data link system, enabling Airbus AiRTHM engineers to deliver maintenance and technical advice both in flight and on the ground.

Benefits include:

■ Enhanced aircraft operational and dispatch reliability
■ Minimised aircraft grounding time
■ Reduced costs
■ Anticipated scheduled maintenance
■ Early delivery of components

The aircraft had flown some 3,000 flights and carried around 1.2 million passengers since being delivered to the airline in 2008. Having all the seats removed from the cabin provided the opportunity to have them reupholstered, replace the carpet and re-laminate the wall panels. Given that the airline operates in the harsh climate of Dubai, their maintenance standards are higher than those required by Airbus or governmental authorities.

One of the key tasks that forms part of MRO activities is the repainting of aircraft, which happens around every seven or eight years of service. In a typical year, an airline the size of Emirates will repaint around 15% of its fleet. Unlike painting a new aircraft, the team must first prepare the aircraft by masking certain areas to protect them from paint, and then the team needs to strip the existing paint and sand all of the external surfaces before finally starting to repaint.

Emirates has recently pioneered an innovation in the A380 repainting process by using a new adhesion promoter which ensures enhanced paint durability and longevity. The colossal nose-to-tail paint job takes 34 employees around 15 days (nearly 6,000 man hours) to repaint just one of more than 90 A380s in its fleet.

Airport case studies: preparing for the arrival of the A380

Dubai (DXB), United Arab Emirates

Based out of Dubai, Emirates has championed the A380 since it launched, putting the super jumbo at the centre of its passenger offering with more than 90 operational aircraft and several more on order. As one of the world's fastest-growing carriers and the largest customer of the A380, the airline helped inaugurate the world's first terminal

LEFT Cargo is unloaded from an Emirates A380 at Heathrow. Trials for a variety of ramp scenarios were simulated and more than 40 pieces of ground servicing equipment were tested before the aircraft entered service. *(Author)*

exclusively designed for the aircraft at Dubai International Airport.

At a cost of some £2.4 billion, it opened with 20 gates designed to service the significant increases in passenger numbers seen at one of the world's biggest hubs. Operating from a purpose-built terminal has sped up boarding times, courtesy of some 58 specifically commissioned airbridges. With the upper door at a height of 8m, some 3m higher than on other aircraft, the bridge's support and lift columns were strengthened. Stabilisers extending out to the right and left were added to make the bridges more secure in case of high winds.

Additional gates have since been added and the airport holds the record for the highest number of A380-capable gates. The terminal's new concourse is spread across 11 floors and also deals with A380 flights to Europe operated by Australia's Qantas airline.

Frankfurt (FRA), Germany

Frankfurt Airport's chairman heralded the A380 as the catalyst in 'a new age in air travel that is likely to spark fierce competition among the leading airports of Europe' as his airport – the third most important passenger hub on the continent – prepared itself to handle the A380.

The arrival of the new aircraft did not necessitate a major upgrade for Frankfurt – the northern runway already met the necessary width and length requirements and taxiways would allow for A380 operations without any problems. Some modifications were made to Frankfurt's Terminals 1 and 2, where up to five gates were upgraded to be capable of serving the A380, in the process ensuring simultaneous passenger boarding on both decks of the A380.

Changi Airport (SIN), Singapore

Singapore Changi Airport became the first

ABOVE Dubai Airport is the first in the world to feature a terminal exclusively designed for the A380. *(Emirates)*

BELOW As one of the world's leading airlines, Lufthansa's expertise not only helped to develop the A380 cockpit and cabin, but also how best to cope with the aircraft on the ground. *(Lufthansa)*

airport outside Europe to welcome the Airbus A380. Compatibility testing took place in late 2005, two years prior to Changi being the host of the inaugural A380 commercial flight.

Early tests also afforded the airport an opportunity to assess the effectiveness and efficiency of their infrastructure, equipment and operating procedures ahead of time.

Fortunately the airport's existing runway – with a length of 4,000m and width of 60m – met the requirements for A380 operations. However, the existing runway shoulders had to be widened by 4.5m on each side to allow the A380 aircraft to operate safely. The aircraft pavements at runway–taxiway and taxiway–taxiway intersections were also widened to allow pilots to comfortably manoeuvre the giant A380 aircraft.

Other parts of the airport's infrastructure that needed modification included passenger gates and baggage carousels which had to be extended to accommodate the increased volumes of luggage.

Besides making modifications to existing infrastructure, new remote aircraft parking stands were built for A380 flights, while further investment was made in protective shields – installed along each side of a taxiway bridge – to contain the effect of the A380 jet blast.

To facilitate passenger movements from the terminal buildings to the airbridges, existing fixed gangways (linking the gate to the airbridge) also had to be modified for A380 compatibility.

John F. Kennedy Airport (JFK), New York

At JFK, some £145m was spent on runway and taxiway modifications alone to accommodate the A380 and planning for the new super jumbo started more than ten years before its first touchdown at the airport in March 2007. A comparable level of investment was made by airlines in the airport's passenger and cargo facilities. One of the biggest challenges faced by JFK was having to relocate a taxiway – with some 58 extensions – that ran around the entire central terminal area.

As a premier US gateway to international traffic and because several foreign carriers had committed to purchase the new aircraft, JFK Airport took the lead for entry of the A380 to the country and were commended in the industry for sharing the lessons learned and best practice surrounding the complexities and implications of modifications made to their facilities.

Miami International Airport (MIA), Florida

Airports had to make wise decisions when preparing for the arrival of the A380. At Miami International Airport, for example, the airport's most southerly runway was specifically chosen as the one preferred to handle the A380, given its proximity to the new A380 gates, the shortest taxi distances (especially in east flow arrivals – east flow is the dominant flow at MIA at 75% of the time), and as the runway that would offer the minimum operational disruption.

Heathrow Airport (LHR), London

A key A380 destination, Heathrow is estimated to have spent more than £600m to reposition taxiways and provide the necessary infrastructure to accommodate the A380 and its passengers.

In order to prepare for the arrival of their fleet of A380s, British Airways Engineering had to complete a series of trials in their facility at Heathrow specifically converted for the aircraft. The trials involved putting the designated maintenance hangars through their paces and Airbus flew in one of its test aircraft to facilitate the trial.

The refurbishment of the four-hangar complex, a landmark 1950s listed building, meant British Airways could welcome the A380 to its engineering base. The team had to overcome several challenges, one of which was to slot the giant aircraft's 24m-high tailfin into the hangar. More than 138 tonnes of steelwork was added to the roof structure to create a slot – an extra notch in height of 3.5m – to allow the A380 tail to pass through. The upgraded state-of-the-art facility means British Airways are able to maintain their own A380 fleet as well as those of other carriers.

Auckland (AKL), New Zealand

Auckland Airport geared up well in advance for the A380, knowing the importance the aircraft's arrival in service would have on the country's travel, tourism and airfreight industries.

The airport and its consulting engineers began work in 1998 to determine what needed to be done to the airport and the staging of necessary developments over time. Modifications included two A380 gates on the international terminal, a remote hard stand being re-dimensioned for A380 services, the addition of a 7.5m asphalt strip down each side of the main runway for the wider overhang of the A380 engines and the widening of taxiway corners.

Los Angeles International (LAX)

By early 2017 LAX was operating 12 gates that can accommodate the A380 and has plans to add six more when the airport's new concourse is completed in 2020. It's a popular hub for the super jumbo, with the likes of Qantas flying some 40 flights per week between LAX and

Sydney, Melbourne and Brisbane, Australia. Qantas isn't the only carrier relying on the A380 – Air France, British Airways, China Southern, Asiana, Emirates and Korean Air also fly the A380 jet to and from LAX.

In a bold move, Qantas recently unveiled a new £24m hangar at LAX big enough to hold and perform maintenance on the world's largest passenger jet. At 480ft × 370ft and 12 storeys tall, it is one of the largest commercial hangars in North America and the only facility in the USA specifically designed for the aircraft. The complex features two aircraft parking pads with walkways directly connecting the jet's doors to the workshop mezzanine level, and a large spare parts facility that includes two vertical lifts to enable efficient delivery of components to the engineering teams. Qantas plans to rent out the facility to other A380 carriers operating at LAX.

ABOVE Heathrow is a key A380 destination and the airport is estimated to have spent more than £600m to reposition taxiways and provide the necessary infrastructure to accommodate the A380. *(Author)*

BELOW A Qatar Airways A380 commences its taxi to the departure runway at Heathrow. *(Author)*

CHAPTER 8

Turnround

OPPOSITE A British Airways A380 arrives at Heathrow's Terminal 5 and the airbridges are attached once on stand. *(Author)*

RIGHT **Air conditioning piping is connected to the aircraft once on stand.** *(Author)*

Introduction

It's a well-known saying in the aviation industry that the highest source of inefficiency in an aircraft's life is its time spent on the ground.

In an age when airlines have to make their assets – the aircraft – work as economically as possible, it's imperative that turnround procedures are super-efficient. The biggest test of a smooth operation comes from handling the biggest aircraft – and they don't come any bigger than the A380. The term 'turnround' refers to the period beginning when a flight arrives at an airport and ending when the aircraft takes off again. During the turnround, a defined series of actions have to be undertaken, involving both airline and airport operations as well as other parties such as ground handlers.

The various ramp service functions – including cleaning, refuelling, essential maintenance, disembarking and boarding

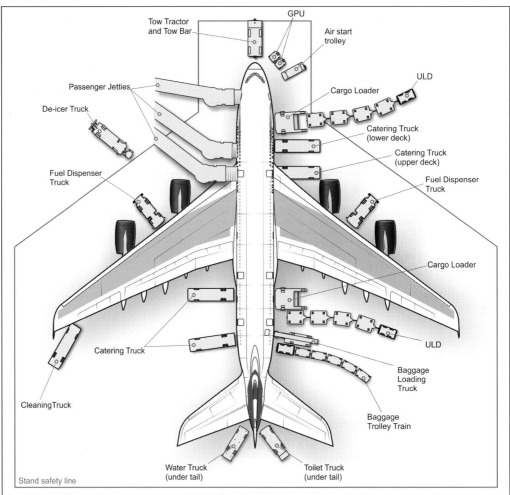

RIGHT **A multitude of different vehicles and service personnel descend on an A380 during the turnround.** *(Roy Scorer)*

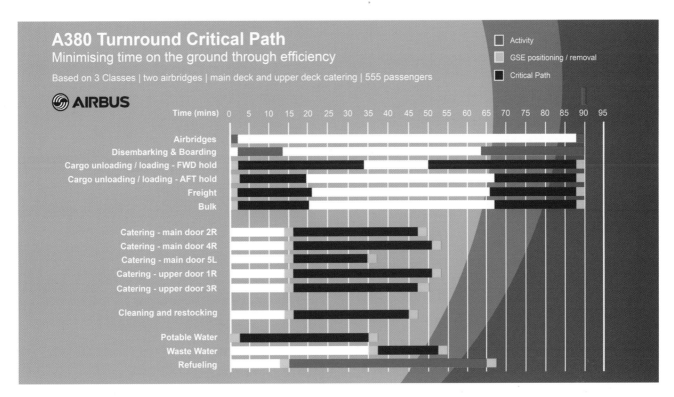

A380 Turnround Critical Path
Minimising time on the ground through efficiency

Based on 3 Classes | two airbridges | main deck and upper deck catering | 555 passengers

AIRBUS

Legend:
- □ Activity
- □ GSE positioning / removal
- ■ Critical Path

Time (mins): 0 5 10 15 20 25 30 35 40 45 50 55 60 65 70 75 80 85 90 95

Activities:
- Airbridges
- Disembarking & Boarding
- Cargo unloading / loading - FWD hold
- Cargo unloading / loading - AFT hold
- Freight
- Bulk
- Catering - main door 2R
- Catering - main door 4R
- Catering - main door 5L
- Catering - upper door 1R
- Catering - upper door 3R
- Cleaning and restocking
- Potable Water
- Waste Water
- Refueling

of passengers and unloading and loading of cargo – are carried out by a combination of airline-supplied services and contracted third parties who work in collaboration to ensure the turnround is carried out safely with speed, efficiency and accuracy.

With around 450–550 seats in multiple classes, the A380 presents a significant challenge to those responsible for meeting the deadlines to prepare the aircraft for its next departure and this has necessitated investment in people, processes and the equipment to make it happen. Flight scheduling has to be carefully managed to cater for regular maintenance checks, but at the same time allowing for maximum aircraft utilisation.

This chapter looks at how airlines cope with super jumbos between flights, including a detailed case study, which tracks a complete turnround of a British Airways A380 at Heathrow.

Critical path

Initial fears that the A380 would take an extended period of time to turnround were soon laid to rest when Airbus, together with partner airlines, looked closely at the critical path planning for the aircraft. This is a common tool used in the aviation industry and identifies all the key tasks that need to be completed within the available time.

Even if disembarking and boarding is limited to two airbridges, Airbus designed the aircraft to ensure it minimised the time of the critical path, meaning it is perfectly feasible for an A380 to be turned round in 90 minutes.

The chart overleaf provides a typical turnround time estimate showing the likely time for ramp activities using standard servicing via the main and upper deck of the aircraft. Actual times may vary due to each airline's specific practices, resources, equipment and operating conditions.

ABOVE Adhering to the turnround schedule is essential and all ramp activities need to be carefully choreographed. *(Author)*

BELOW The A380 was designed to operate using much of the same ground servicing equipment as that already in use at airports around the world. *(Author)*

1	Passenger handling	
	Assumes 555 passengers: 22 in first class/96 in business class/437 in economy	
	All passengers deplane and board the aircraft	
	2 airbridges used at doors M2L and U1L	
	Equipment positioning main deck + opening door	3 mins
	Closing door and equipment removal main deck	3 mins
	Equipment positioning upper deck + opening door	4 mins
	Closing door and equipment removal upper deck	4 mins
	Assumes no passengers with reduced mobility on board	
	Deplaning – assuming priority for premium passengers	
	356 passengers at door M2L (22 first class and 334 economy)	
	199 passengers at door U1L (96 business class and 103 economy)	
	Deplaning rate for passengers	25 per min per door
	Boarding	
	356 passengers at door M2L (22 first class and 334 economy)	
	199 passengers at door U1L (96 business class and 103 economy)	
	Boarding rate	15 per min per door
	Last passenger seating allowance and head counting	4 mins
2	Cargo	
	2 cargo loaders and 1 belt loader	
	Opening door and equipment positioning	2.5 mins
	Equipment removal and closing door	2.5 mins
	100% cargo exchange	
	Forward cargo compartment: 20 containers	
	Aft cargo compartment: 16 containers	
	Bulk cargo compartment: 1,000kg	
	Container unloading/loading times	
	Unloading	1.2 mins/container
	Loading	1.4 mins/container
	Bulk unloading/loading times:	
	Unloading	110kg/min
	Loading	95kg/min
3	Refuelling	
	242,700 litres at 40psig	
	Dispenser positioning and connection	8 mins
	Disconnection and dispenser removal	8 mins
4	Catering	
	3 main deck catering trucks and 1 upper deck catering truck	
	Main deck equipment positioning and door opening	5 mins
	Main deck closing door and equipment removal	3 mins
	Upper deck equipment positioning and door opening	9 mins
	Upper deck closing door and equipment removal	4 mins
	Full-size trolley equivalent (FSTE) to unload and load: 78 FSTE	
	28 FSTE at door M2R	
	16 FSTE at door M4R	
	23 FSTE at door U1R	
	11 FSTE at door M5L	
	Time for trolley exchange	1.5 mins per FSTE
	Time for trolley exchange via lift	2 mins per FSTE
4	Ground handling/Service	
	Start of operations	
	Airbridges	
	Other equipment	1 min
	Air conditioning: up to 4 hoses	
	Ground Power Unit (GPU): up to 4 × 90kVA	
	Potable water servicing: 100% uplift, 1,700 litres	
	Waste water servicing: draining and rinsing – there are four waste tanks, two upper deck tanks and two main deck tanks	

Disembarking and boarding

For airlines operating wide-body aircraft, one of the most challenging elements of the turnround critical path is boarding and deboarding of passengers and when those numbers are consistently above 500, the significance of this aspect is clear.

With passenger capacity some 35% higher than the Boeing 747-400, the A380 offers a productivity step-change but Airbus knew it would be essential to try to keep turnround times to 90 minutes and made this one of the critical design parameters of the aircraft.

Boarding currently takes place using either two (one servicing the main and one the upper deck) or three airbridges (two for the main deck and one for the upper deck). There were initial concerns that in order to ensure competitive turnround times for the A380, airports needed to provide at least three passenger bridges but experience has shown that this is not necessarily the case and that the time required for boarding and deboarding the A380 via passenger bridges connected to door M1L and M2L on the main deck are similar to the Boeing 747-400. Wider aisles and unobstructed access at door M2 greatly aid the process. With the critical boarding path on the main deck, direct access to the A380's upper deck is not an operational necessity to achieve short turnround times.

That said, the addition of a third bridge offers significant potential in terms of passenger comfort and product differentiation. For most airlines, the ability to offer their largely premium-class passengers direct upper-deck access to the aircraft is seen as a unique offering. Airports also realise that the level of service provided to passengers can be a decisive argument in remaining competitive. If an airport currently offers two bridges, the airlines' preferred choice is to have one of them upgraded to reach the upper deck. The feasibility of upgrading existing stands for upper-deck access largely varies from airport to airport and depends mainly on the constraints imposed by the existing gate layout.

It was not just passenger numbers that demanded further consideration – the equipment needed for getting passengers on and off the super jumbo took some clever engineering.

As mentioned, the upper door of the A380 is at a height of 8m, 3m higher than on other aircraft, so the airbridge's support and lift columns had to be strengthened. Higher winds at that height meant stabilisers – extending out to the left and right – also had to be added. There were further challenges when using all three doors of the aircraft. The proximity of the airbridges to one another meant the tunnels were only about a metre apart, so engineers developed an anti-collision system.

ABOVE At most airports, passengers can board the A380 using airbridges to both the main and upper decks.
(Air France)

Cargo

The A380 has 184m³ of cargo hold space and this is divided between separate forward and aft holds. The lower deck forward cargo compartment is 17.4m in length and can accommodate 20 LD3 containers or 7

BELOW Positioning the airbridges has to be done carefully given their proximity to one another.

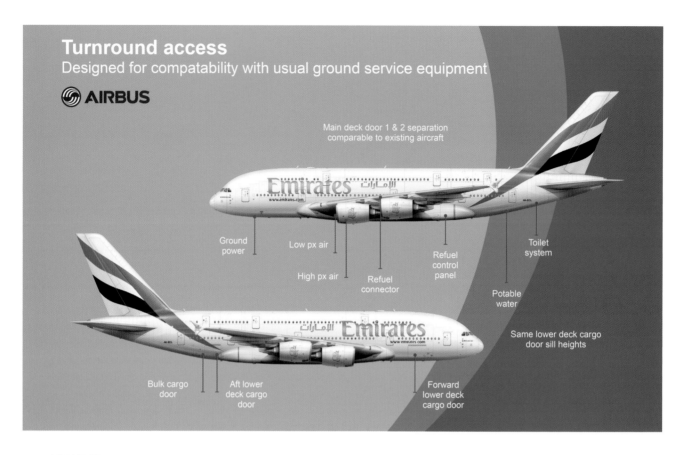

Turnround access
Designed for compatability with usual ground service equipment

AIRBUS

Main deck door 1 & 2 separation
comparable to existing aircraft

Ground power

Low px air

High px air

Refuel connector

Refuel control panel

Toilet system

Potable water

Same lower deck cargo door sill heights

Bulk cargo door

Aft lower deck cargo door

Forward lower deck cargo door

ABOVE The upper deck airbridge must reach a height of 8m and needs additional stabilisers. *(Author)*

RIGHT Unloading of the forward cargo hold on a British Airways A380 at Heathrow. *(Author)*

BELOW The forward cargo hold is emptied of containers and inspected prior to loading of outbound cargo. *(Author)*

pallets. The lower deck aft cargo compartment is T-shaped with the first (narrower) section measuring 9.7m in length and the second 8.2m. Combined, they can accommodate 16 LD3 containers or 6 pallets. Behind this sits the lower deck bulk cargo compartment, measuring 2.8m in length. The containers with passenger baggage are brought to the aircraft from the airport's baggage-handling facility and loaded using scissor-lift platforms. Smaller bulk items are loaded using a mobile conveyor unit.

Technical checks

Technical procedures are very similar between the different airlines that fly the A380 and when one arrives on stand – a British Airways one at London Heathrow in this instance – a team of licensed engineers and approved technicians head to the aircraft to deal with any issues ahead of the next flight.

The team is made up of personnel from the airline's Line Maintenance Engineering Department as well as the Cabin Team, and they are allocated to attend to various inbound aircraft on any one day.

Depending on the level of maintenance called for by the airline's Planning Department, the engineers will always carry out a thorough walk-around, check and replenish the engine oil levels, clean the landing gear oleos and attend to anything inside the aircraft that pertains to the aircraft's technical log.

The log contains any system or observed faults experienced by the incoming crew to alert maintenance teams of work that may be required before the next flight or defects that may be deferred. Any deferred defects comply with the appropriate documentation such as the MEL. The MEL details the minimum equipment needed to operate the flight safely as well as any inoperative systems that are noted on the CDL and can be deferred and rectified at a later point in time. Using this system ensures the aircraft will not receive its 'fit for flight' release documents unless all log entries have been accounted for.

The engineer accesses the aircraft's e-log via the onboard maintenance terminal (OMT), located behind the First Officer's seat.

The OMT is used by both Engineering and

Cabin teams to interrogate aircraft systems and by using the real-time monitoring mode, they are able to see exactly what a valve or pump is doing versus its commanded and/or selected position – this aids in fault-finding and fault isolation.

The aircraft automatically produces a post-flight report (PFR) on each landing which further assists the engineers to address and rectify any faults. The OMT also helps in carrying out numerous system tests and when used in conjunction with the electronic aircraft maintenance manual, circuit breakers can be 'pulled' and tagged directly via the OMT.

Finally, the OMT is very useful during departures as a third screen to 'transfer' faults on to, thereby minimising flight crew distraction – for example any current ECAM message can be relayed to the OMT for engineers to subsequently rectify while the flight crew remain focused on the task at hand.

Further routine/inspections during a daily, weekly, monthly and an A Check consist of the following:

- Tyre pressures
- Brake pack wear indicator pins
- Hydraulic fluid levels
- Crew and cabin oxygen system levels
- APU oil level
- Wing and trim tank water drains
- Static port cleaning
- Cargo hold inspections
- Fire extinguishing system test
- Printer paper complement

ABOVE Baggage containers are quickly unloaded and transferred to the baggage hall where they are collected by the arriving passengers. *(Author)*

- Flight crew headset complement, cleanliness and earphone security
- External lighting including taxi cameras
- Internal lighting including emergency systems
- P30 sense line moisture removal
- Engine starter servicing
- Variable frequency generator servicing (ground idle check start required for leaks)
- Hydraulic pump case drain filter replacements (ground idle check start required for leaks)
- Engine fuel filter replacements (ground idle check start required for leaks)
- Cabin and galley ventilation filter replacements
- Wine chiller filter replacements
- Lavatory sink strainer replacements
- Toilet bowl and associated drain pipe acidic cleaning.

Other tasks can include:
- Wheel and brake unit replacements
- Bird strike inspections
- Landing gear oleo pressure and dimension checks.

The cabin team will go through the cabin log and attend to any inbound defects and also attempt to clear any additional deferred defects (ADDs). Typical tasks include issues relating to:

- Ovens
- Beverage makers
- Seats in all classes
- Cabin attendant seats
- In-flight entertainment and uploading of new content
- Cabin internal make-up (side walls and ceiling panels).

Catering

The catering process is by far the longest component of the A380 turnround timing and distributing the significant number of containers and trolleys across all the galleys on the main and upper decks in the different areas is the critical path that ultimately determines the length of the turnround.

Airbus strongly recommends to its customer airlines that the A380's upper deck galleys be replenished using the upper deck doors. Upper-deck catering significantly reduces the catering critical path and Airbus estimates that use of just one upper deck catering vehicle cuts the turnround time to less than that required for a Boeing 747.

To make the most of these gains in turnround time requires airline catering companies to invest in specialised scissor trucks capable of reaching the doorsills, which are 8m above the tarmac.

The process can be undertaken using the main deck only, with standard catering vehicles being employed and the catering team relying on catering lifts between the main and upper deck – at doors M2 and M5 – to move the containers to the upper deck. Taking this approach results in a minimum turnround time of 126 minutes rather than 90 minutes.

If the galley door on the upper deck is catered via a dedicated vehicle interfacing directly, the total time for the catering process is significantly reduced. Direct catering of other galleys on the upper deck is also possible, but it does not contribute to a reduction in total catering time, as these galleys are not normally within the critical path of the process.

When an A380 arrives it is stripped of all the catering trolleys and equipment, including reusable crockery and cutlery. These are returned to the supplier for washing and sterilisation. The trolleys

RIGHT Used food trolleys are unloaded onto one of the service trucks before catering supplies can be replenished.
(Author)

LEFT Catering trucks access both the main and upper deck using a scissor lift mechanism. *(Author)*

also undergo safety inspections to check that they are functioning properly.

For outbound flights, catering suppliers are required to orchestrate the assembly of meals according to specifications provided by the airlines based on forecasts of passenger numbers on any given flight.

Refuelling

Refuelling the A380 is a fully automated process, with the operator required to simply enter the amount of fuel requested on the refuel/defuel control panel. This is located in the aircraft's underbelly. The amount of fuel uploaded depends on a variety of factors, including how much fuel remains after the previous flight, the take-off weight, the flight plan as well as the expected weather conditions for the sector.

Refuelling of an A380 happens in the same way as most other commercial aircraft. Each airline is contracted to a fuel company and one of their dispenser vehicles arrives on stand at a designated time that fits into the critical path.

The operator positions his vehicle under the aircraft's left wing and first connects an anti-static device – the extensive flow of fuel can generate static, which can create a deadly spark (jet fuel is kerosene-based, and much more flammable than petrol). Next, he connects his vehicle to the stand's underground hydrant, then uses the vehicle's lift platform to reach a panel located on the underside of the wing and connects two large refuelling pipes.

The fuel in the hydrant is pressurised and the vehicle is used not only to filter and meter the fuel, but also to depressurise it from 150psi to 50psi. The advantage of hydrant fuelling over the use of a tanker is the removal from

BELOW The refuelling truck arrives on stand with a single operator responsible for refuelling an A380. *(Author)*

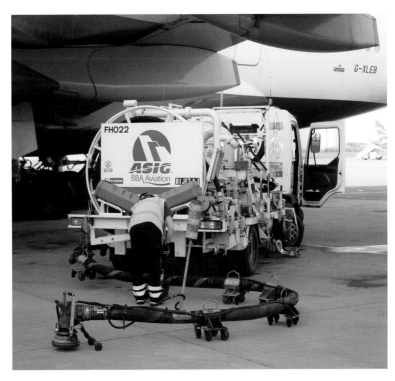

an already congested stand of a large vehicle and the speed and volume of fuel that can be transferred. Also, given that an A380 has a capacity of 320,000 litres and a tanker only has a capacity of 40,000 litres, it would take eight tankers to refuel an empty aircraft.

Filling the super jumbo can take up to 90 minutes (45 if fuelling using both sides) at a rate of about 4,000 litres per minute and British Airways' refuelling contractor, ASIG, move about 3,000,000 gallons of fuel every day at Heathrow alone.

With everything connected, the operator checks the fuel panel on the aircraft, enters the total required fuel load and starts the refuelling process, relying on the A380 complex fuel system to handle distribution to the 11 different tanks automatically. The calculated final load and fuel distribution will ensure a properly trimmed and balanced aircraft.

The operator does not leave the aircraft during the refuel and holds firmly in his hand what is known in the industry as a 'deadman device'. This is one of a number of clever safety features. He releases the lever every now and then for a brief moment in order to confirm a continuous flow and that he is – well – still alive. If he let go of the deadman device, the system would immediately stop the refuelling process.

Quality control and contamination issues take up much of the operator's time – the dispensers are fitted with filtering, monitoring and recording equipment. Once the required amount is filled, the operator disconnects the pipes from the wings, closes the panel, removes the ground pipe and static device, prints a receipt and gets the engineer to sign it before starting the process all over again on another aircraft.

During fuelling, air and vapour are displaced

from the aircraft fuel tanks but is expelled via vent points on the aircraft's wings.

Weight and balance

As is the case with all aircraft, a clear set of rules and methods are used to ensure there is no excess weight and the distribution of the load being carried is balanced. If these factors are not considered, the safety of the flight is put at risk as the pilot's ability to manoeuvre and control the aircraft may be impaired.

All aircraft have a maximum allowable weight limit – as documented by the manufacturer – that cannot be exceeded and airlines spend much time planning and calculating the expected load of a departing aircraft. They factor in all aspects including passengers, baggage, cargo, crew, fuel and onboard supplies such as catering.

Planners consider three key weights when preparing for a departure:

- The Maximum Take-Off Weight (MTOW): 575 tonnes
  This has to be adjusted for local conditions based on the length of the runways, prevailing weather conditions, temperature, barometric pressure, wind direction and speed.
- The Maximum Landing Weight (MLW): 395 tonnes

This is considered to ensure that the stress limits for the aircraft's landing gear are not exceeded. Attention is also given to the length of the landing runway which may limit the distance the aircraft has in which to slow down and stop.

- The Maximum Zero Fuel Weight (MZFW): 369 tonnes
  This is the maximum structural loading on the wing root structure that may not be exceeded and ensures the aircraft is not too heavy for the airframe. The total weight of the aircraft as prepared for the flight, minus the weight of the fuel equals the MZFW.

The final load information is then compared against these weights before the load sheet is approved and handed to the ground handling team who must ensure that the aircraft is loaded exactly in accordance with the load plan, thereby ensuring the aircraft is suitably balanced for flight. The loading of fuel and cargo is generally arranged to ensure that if there are any last-minute changes to the payload or passenger numbers, a new calculation is performed and uploaded to the aircraft. Changes to the optimum TOW centre of gravity are resolved by transferring fuel to rebalance the aircraft and return the CG to the ideal position.

ABOVE An Etihad A380 taxis at Heathrow Airport en route to runway 27R for departure. *(Author)*

Pre-flight inspection

Prior to boarding the aircraft, the A380's flight crew meets the ground engineer who briefs them on the aircraft's serviceability. The flight crew also follows a set of standard operating procedures (SOP) related to the exterior walk around, the focus of which is to:

- Obtain a global assessment of the aircraft status – checking for any missing parts or panels. They consult the CDL for dispatch, and evaluate any operational consequences.
- Ensure that the main control surfaces are in the appropriate position compared to the surface control levers.
- Check that there are no leaks.
- Check the condition of the essential visible sensors, such as pitot and static probes.
- Observe any abnormal condition of the landing gear:
  - Cuts, wear or cracks on wheels and tyres
  - Condition of the brakes
  - Length of shock absorbers.
- Observe any abnormal condition of the engines:
  - Fan blades, turbine exhaust, engine cowl and pylon condition
  - Access door should be closed
  - Thrust reverser door condition.

Once they are satisfied, the flight crew board the aircraft and make final preparations for take-off.

BELOW The fan blades of the engines are thoroughly checked as part of the pre-flight inspection. *(Waldo van der Waal)*

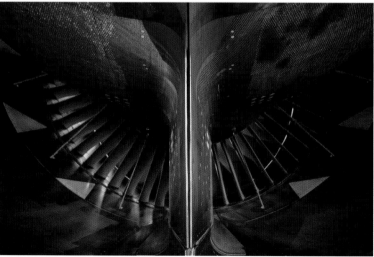

De-icing

A build-up of ice can jam control surfaces (rudder, flaps, ailerons, elevators and slats), preventing them from moving properly, hence de-icing is essential, the trigger for which is determined by the specifications set by the airframe manufacturer.

Ice can also cause critical control surfaces to be rough and uneven, disrupting smooth airflow and significantly limiting the ability of the wing to generate lift. In addition, should large pieces of ice separate when the aircraft is in flight, they can be ingested into the engines and cause a catastrophic failure.

The biggest challenge when it comes to de-icing an A380 is that the ground servicing equipment must be capable of reaching heights of up to approximately 24m. The surface areas to be de-iced are vast, as shown in the following table.

Wing top surface (both sides)	723m²
Wingtip devices (both inside and outside surfaces (both sides)	10m²
Horizontal tailplane surface (both sides)	186m²
Vertical tailplane (both sides)	230m²
Fuselage top surface (top third – 120° arc)	497m²
Nacelle and pylon (all engines – top third – 120° arc)	112m²
Total de-iced area	1,758m²

De-icing involves the application of chemicals that not only de-ice, but also remain on the surface to delay the re-formation of ice for a certain period of time. De-icing techniques are also used to ensure that engine inlets and various sensors on the outside of the aircraft are clear of ice or snow.

De-icing is typically done by spraying aircraft with a de-icing fluid based on propylene glycol, similar to ethylene glycol anti-freeze used in some car engine coolants. De-icing fluids are always applied heated and diluted.

The de-icing fluid is sprayed through a nozzle that can be adjusted to give a moderate jet of fluid on to the contaminated area and then a short time later the pressure is increased to use the hydraulic force to flush off loosened deposits.

Once an aircraft has been de-iced, it is

imperative that it leaves the gate within a set time limit known as the 'hold-over time' otherwise there is the risk that the freezing conditions will create more ice and nullify the impact of the de-icing. Aircraft that haven't left within the required window and have to be de-iced again add to congestion and impact on airport efficiency.

Pushback

With the aircraft ready for departure, the captain will call for pushback, the procedure whereby the aircraft is actually pushed backwards away from the gate by external power, rather than manoeuvring under its own power. Pushbacks are carried out by special low-profile vehicles called tractors or tugs.

Pushback tractors use a low-profile design to fit under the nose of the aircraft and need to be capable of generating significant levels of traction to move large passenger aircraft; 50-tonne tractors are common at major airports and can handle the A380 in most conditions. In the case of adverse traction – where the ramp may be contaminated or the slope is an issue – a 70-tonne tractor may be required. The driver's cabin can be raised for increased visibility when reversing, and lowered to fit under the aircraft. The procedure is subject to ground control confirming it is clear to commence the procedure. Once clearance is obtained, the pilot communicates with the pushback tractor driver (or a ground handler walking alongside the aircraft in some cases) to start the operation. To communicate, a headset is connected to the aircraft near the nose gear.

The same ground handler temporarily installs a bypass pin into the nose gear to disconnect it from the aircraft's normal steering mechanism. The pin prevents the aircraft from being mishandled by the tug; when overstressed, the shear pin will snap, disconnecting the bar from the nose gear to prevent damage to the aircraft and tug.

The A380 is designed with means for conventional towing or towbarless towing and both methods are in use at airports around the world. The aircraft can be towed or pushed at

maximum ramp weight with engines at zero or up to idle thrust using a towbar attached to the nose gear leg. The towbar fitting is installed at the front of the leg and an optional towing fitting – for towing from the rear of the nose gear leg – is available.

Conventional tugs use a towbar to connect the tug to the nose landing gear of the aircraft, the towbar acting as a large lever to rotate the nose landing gear. It must have sufficient length to place the tug far enough away to avoid hitting the aircraft, as well as to provide adequate leverage to facilitate turns. The towbar for an A380 rides on its own wheels, which in turn are attached to a hydraulic jacking mechanism that can lift the towbar to the correct height to mate to the aircraft and the tug.

Towbarless (TBL) tractors do not use a towbar. They scoop up the nosewheel and lift it off the ground, allowing the tug to manoeuvre the aircraft. The main advantage of a TBL tug is its simplicity but, additionally, operators are spared from having to maintain a range of different towbars. Connecting the tug directly to the aircraft's landing gear – instead of through a towbar – allows tug operators to have better control and responsiveness when manoeuvring. This is certainly advantageous when moving an aircraft the size of the A380.

Once the pushback is completed, the towbar or scoop is disconnected or disengaged, and the bypass pin is removed and the aircraft can start taxiing towards the runway for departure under its own power.

ABOVE A conventional tug pushes back an Etihad A380 from its stand at Heathrow's Terminal 4. *(Author)*

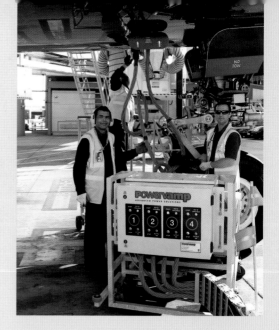

It's a Thursday evening in the USA and British Airways flight BA268 departs Terminal B at Los Angeles International Airport (LAX) at 19:55 local time. This Airbus A380 (registration G-XLEB) follows a route across southern California, Nevada, Utah, Wyoming, South and North Dakota, before passing over the border with Canada heading across Ontario, Quebec and Newfoundland and then routing across the Atlantic and on to London's Heathrow Airport.

This is one of the airline's most popular routes served by the A380 and on board are 440 passengers. Following a short hold in the air traffic control stack, the aircraft lands at 16:10 on runway 27L and enjoys a short taxi to Heathrow's Terminal 5C, arriving on stand 564 just before 16:30 on Friday afternoon.

BA's Turnround Manager (TRM) for this flight is Mark Chappell. He has the task of ensuring this aircraft is efficiently transformed into the BA11 flight from Heathrow to Singapore and he has just three hours to make it happen. The A380 can be prepared in 90 minutes if needed, but as this is the aircraft's home base and BA's extensive engineering facilities are on hand, more time is provided to the engineering team to carry out scheduled servicing tasks.

Mark's job is not an easy one. He has to co-ordinate the activities of some 75 different people who will be smoothly choreographed to work on the aircraft over the next 180 minutes, ensuring an on-time departure. Not only is there pressure to get the aircraft away on schedule, but doing so means the stand is freed up as planned for the next inbound aircraft.

With the wheel chocks in place, the engine shut down and the aircraft connected to the ground power unit, the three airbridges move in sequence, enabling the passengers to disembark, with priority given to those travelling in the airline's premium classes.

Next into the mix is the baggage handling team who are quick off the mark and use special scissor-lift trucks that enable them to reach up to open the A380's front and rear hold doors. They unload a variety of items, including passenger bags, express handling, mail, palletised cargo and loose items like prams and golf clubs.

It isn't possible to simultaneously offload the bags and cargo and at the same time de-cater because the required vehicles need to park in almost the same position to carry out their duties. Consequently, the hold is usually cleared first, the respective doors closed, and then the high-lift catering trucks come alongside the service doors.

On schedule, a team from catering supplier Gate Gourmet clear the galleys by offloading catering trolleys from both the main and upper decks. They then begin the process of resupplying the aircraft with more than 1,000 meals and 2,000 beverages as passengers will enjoy both dinner and lunch en route to Singapore.

At the same time it's the airline's technical team who access the aircraft for a routine check. BA engineer Khalid Murad performs a visual

FAR RIGHT Ground power is connected as soon as the aircraft arrives on stand.
(Author)

BELOW BA268 from Los Angeles touches down at Heathrow.
(Author)

FAR LEFT A member of the ground team uses a platform to access the rear cargo door. (*Author*)

LEFT Scissor lift vehicles move in to unload the containers from the hold. (*Author*)

inspection of the aircraft by walking round the exterior and then proceeds to oversee a routine service requirement on the No. 3 engine's variable frequency generator (VFG). The VFG is driven off the accessory gearbox and is in essence the component that provides AC electrical power to the aircraft systems. The team performs a filter removal, inspection for particulates and an oil change. The engine is then started to accomplish a generator 'on-line' function and to check for any leaks to disturbed pipes and the filter housing. All work carried out on the aircraft is in accordance with the manufacturer's maintenance manual and relevant company procedures.

Inside the aircraft the Cabin Team deal with a troublesome seat in the Club World cabin, while

ABOVE Bulk items in the rear cargo compartment include prams and oversize items. (*Author*)

FAR LEFT BA engineer Khalid Murad runs through his checklist in the cockpit. (*Author*)

LEFT A routine service on the No. 3 engine's variable frequency generator is attended to during the turnround. (*Author*)

TOP A team of cleaners works quickly and efficiently to prepare the economy cabin. *(Author)*

ABOVE The cleaning team also prepares the aircraft's Club World cabin. *(Author)*

BELOW The A380's refuelling panel. *(Airbus)*

another engineer deals with a problematic toilet. When the engineering teams are finished and Khalid is satisfied, he completes the technical and cabin logs.

Meanwhile, a team of cleaners, supplied by contractor Omniserv, swarm through the various cabins, clearing rubbish, cleaning the toilets, vacuuming the carpets and wiping down tables. They then set about restocking supplies including everything from in-flight magazines, headphones, water bottles, amenity kits and comfort items to bedding, toiletries, socks and headrest covers for 14 First Class, 97 Club World, 55 World Traveller Plus and 303 World Traveller passengers.

A vehicle – known to those on the tarmac as the 'honey wagon' – arrives to discharge the effluent from four toilet waste tanks and 1,300 litres of water are added to the A380's fresh water tanks. Meanwhile, refuelling contractor ASIG loads 180 tonnes of fuel into the aircraft's fuel tanks, 1.5 tonnes of which will be used for taxi out to the end of the runway alone. Generally speaking, aircraft are partially refuelled before the pilots report for duty. They are then topped up to the captain's requirements shortly before departure.

Check-in and baggage delivery through to the aircraft is handled by British Airways. The passenger bags are loaded and the airline's central load control provide a loading instruction report. The TRM briefs the loader and cross-checks against the list. The A380 can accommodate 32 baggage containers and those passengers with connections as well as those in the premium classes are packed in separate containers which will be unloaded first on arrival into Singapore.

With an hour to go, no further passengers are accepted for the flight and shortly thereafter the cabin crew and pilots arrive at the aircraft to make the final preparations in the cabins and flight deck respectively.

British Airways require all passengers to have cleared security at least 35 minutes prior to departure. Mark has to deal with a passenger who has a mobility issue and is running late to the gate for boarding. He's informed the customer is on his way but the clock is ticking to departure. He checks to see where the passenger's bags are located in the hold in case they need to be offloaded but he makes it – just in time to board. Everything builds in the last 20 minutes and this is undoubtedly the most pressurised time with a variety of issues that need to be dealt with quickly – everything from a lost passport to a delayed inbound flight – with passengers desperate to make their connection.

The outbound flight has 468 passengers booked on it, leaving just a single spare seat in the economy cabin – clearly another very popular route for BA's customers. In the end, five passengers are delayed on a connecting flight, so the aircraft departs with 463 customers, 4 flight crew and 22 cabin crew. The aircraft is full in First, Club, World Traveller Plus and there are just six spare seats in economy. The final weights of everything in the cabin and the hold are:

- Passengers, crew and cabin bags .... 38 tonnes
- Catering .... 7.3 tonnes
- Water .... 1.3 tonnes
- Baggage in the hold .... 7.3 tonnes
- Cargo in the hold .... 6.2 tonnes

When the final passenger, freight and fuel statistics are finalised, the airline's load control team produces a computerised loadsheet. With boarding complete, Mark makes one final check that everything is in order and hands a copy of the final paperwork for the flight – including the passenger information list and cargo manifest – to Captain Julian Warren. Sitting alongside him is Senior First Officer Marjolein van Deth. Given the length of the sector, on board the A380 the flight crew team also includes Captain Graeme Coombs and Senior First Officer Steven Tucker. The doors are closed and the three airbridges carefully retracted in reverse order.

At precisely the right time, the ground power is disconnected and the chocks removed. Captain Warren receives departure clearance from ATC and calls for pushback. Ground staff walk out on either side of the aircraft to ensure the wingtips are clear and give the thumbs up to the driver of the powerful Douglas TBL–600 towbarless tractor.

This vehicle is designed to cradle the aircraft's nose landing gear and with the flick of a switch in the cab, the cradle lift – capable

of supporting up to 48 tonnes – effortlessly scoops up the nosewheels and eases the giant A380 off the stand and away from the terminal to one of Heathrow's taxiways. At the same time, one excited author enjoys a once-in-a-lifetime ride inside the tractor.

BA's critical path system is called the Precision Time Schedule (PTS) and the efforts of the turnround team, led by Mark, live up to the name. BA11 departs dead on time from the gate and heads towards Heathrow's 27R runway for departure. On Saturday afternoon it arrives – four minutes early – into Singapore's Changi Airport, where the entire turnround process happens again. In the five days that follow, BA's A380 G-XLEB completes return flights from Heathrow to Boston and San Francisco before departing for Manila for a five-week-long scheduled maintenance check.

TOP The BA11 is pushed back from its stand by a towbarless tractor. *(Author)*

ABOVE The A380 is all set for its flight to Singapore, with the crew taking departure instructions from the airport's air traffic control tower in the background. *(Author)*

CHAPTER 9

Epilogue

OPPOSITE The interest from passengers in flying the A380 encouraged Airbus to launch and promote a dedicated website (iflyA380.com) – an innovative booking assistant that opens the door to the world of the iconic double-decker. *(Airbus)*

Market challenges

When the A380 first launched, several airlines jumped on the bandwagon but the momentum Airbus was expecting by way of new orders has failed to materialise in recent years and some of those all-important early orders may not materialise. Qantas, for example, may reduce its initial order from 20 to 12 aircraft. With a diminishing backlog, the initial projections of 1,200 aircraft to be built over a 20-year horizon for the overall market now seem hugely optimistic. Meanwhile, Singapore Airlines – the second biggest customer for the A380 – has announced it will surrender the lease on four of its oldest Airbus A380 super jumbo jets, confirming that the first airline to operate the biggest passenger jets doesn't want to keep the earliest-delivered planes of the model on its fleet. The airline will, however, take delivery of three new A380s by March 2018 as it seeks to operate a young fleet of planes that require less maintenance.

With some airlines scaling back and pressure on other orders, there is even greater significance on the Emirates relationship, with the majority of remaining orders destined for the Middle Eastern carrier.

It is worth noting that the aircraft entered service at the same time as the global recession struck and in the cash-strapped period that followed, the risk-averse boards at many airlines were reluctant to be seen spending £340m on a single aircraft.

Industry trends in recent years show a change in preference by many of the world's airlines to gravitate towards smaller, more fuel-efficient twin-engine long-haul aircraft like Airbus' own A350 and Boeing's 787, with four-engine aircraft becoming a tough sell because of their high fuel consumption. Even Boeing's 747-400 bore the brunt of the switch in a segment they had monopolised for years.

The slowdown will necessitate a temporary cut in production at Toulouse for 2018 – down to just one jet a month from the four originally envisaged for the programme – and questions began to be raised about how many of the remaining orders Airbus had on its books that could potentially fall through.

Despite the cuts, Airbus have publicly committed themselves to the A380 and believe it is here to stay. 'We are maintaining, innovating and investing in the A380, keeping the aircraft the favourite of passengers, the airlines and airports – today and in the future,' said Fabrice Brégier, Airbus President and CEO.

Uncertainty remains about the overall project's profitability, with indications that the recurring cost is being covered but the initial £17.2 billion investment in development looking unlikely to be recouped. Airbus will be frustrated at not being able to develop interest in the A380 from airlines in North America and has been looking at creative ways to market the aircraft, particularly in Asia. The challenge will be to secure new orders soon, given the lengthy lead times in the supply chain.

Capacity constraints and larger aircraft

For many years, Airbus has based much of its rationale for the A380 on the fact that airports are – or eventually will – become so crowded that the only way to meet the industry's demand will be with larger aircraft. It is here that Airbus might just have a point. Air traffic doubles every 15 years, and today 90% of long-haul passengers are travelling through 55 hub cities around the world. 'The A380 is the best aircraft to capture peak demand, while also relieving airport congestion and boosting hub operations,' explained John Leahy, the Chief Operating Officer at Airbus Commercial Aircraft.

At one of the world's most congested and capacity-constrained airports, Heathrow, recent

BELOW Thai Airways successfully operate the A380 between London Terminal 2 and Bangkok, with 12 seats in first class, 60 in business and 435 in economy. *(Airbus)*

passenger growth figures are attributed to larger aircraft. At the end of March 2017, Heathrow announced that larger aircraft carrying more passengers drove a 5.5% growth in passenger numbers, resulting in a record of 5.27 million passengers in a single month at the west London hub. Look across the tarmac at Heathrow and the impact of the A380 is clear to see, with the aircraft utilised by British Airways, Emirates, Etihad Airways, Malaysia Airlines, Qantas, Qatar Airways, Singapore Airlines and Thai Airways.

The airport has seen a steady rise in the number of passengers – currently more than 7 million – who either arrive or depart on an A380. Destinations include Los Angeles, Singapore, Johannesburg, Seoul and Dubai.

British Airways has used the A380 to consolidate frequencies and release valuable slots for new destinations. Up until the summer of 2013, BA operated three daily Boeing 747 flights on the London to Los Angeles route. This was replaced with a twice-daily A380 service which offered the same seat capacity, but lowered the daily trip operating cost by nearly 20%. This consolidation offers more capacity at the peak time when passengers want to travel. In addition, BA A380s are configured to accommodate 5% more premium passengers, leading to higher overall revenue than on its Boeing 747s. Beyond the improvement in efficiency, freeing up a valuable slot for new route development was a key benefit for an airline operating at such a constrained airport.

Airbus has said it is confident the aircraft will see fresh demand as congestion limits the number of slots available at major hub airports and as relatively weak oil prices boost its economics.

Many eggs in the Emirates basket

It's fair to say that much of the aircraft's future hinges on the ongoing success at the Middle East's biggest airline. As the aircraft's largest customer, Emirates have made the A380 the backbone of their fleet since taking their first delivery back in 2008. Some industry critics believe the Emirates relationship is so key that should they fail to place another big order for the aircraft within the next three years, it could be a hammer blow to the wider A380 programme.

ABOVE In January 2017 Etihad Airways doubled its A380 capacity to New York by introducing its second daily service between the UAE capital and JFK. *(Airbus)*

BELOW The A380 is a regular sight at airports the world over – as this line-up of tailplanes clearly shows. *(Airbus)*

BOTTOM Qatar Airways first started operating the A380 in September 2015, six years after placing its initial order. *(Airbus)*

ABOVE The Emirates
A380 now flies to more
than 40 destinations
around the world, with
more being added all
the time. (Airbus)

Consider also that Emirates themselves are not immune to international politics and issues, like a clampdown by US officials on travel from Muslim countries, Brexit and a rise in European terrorism. These issues have all put pressure on the airline's bottom line and raised questions about its ability – and desire – to go ahead with the remaining A380s it has on order. There are also question marks about space constraints at Dubai Airport and how it might cope with yet more A380s.

Given the scale of the commitment from Emirates to the A380, a slowdown in demand from the airline will undoubtedly mean bad news for Airbus. If the carrier cannot fill the super jumbo, it could remove some of the rationale for operating such a large fleet of A380s, turning Emirates towards a competitor aircraft such as Boeing's large wide-body 777X for future orders.

That said, airlines the world over have carefully observed the Emirates strategy and many will be seeking to emulate their dominant position on some of the world's busiest long-haul routes, and using the A380 to do so

BELOW Airbus staff
celebrate the delivery
of the first Emirates
A380 in 2008. (Airbus)

provides not only the capacity but also the opportunity to offer competitive fares. In July 2017 news emerged that Emirates was in talks about the purchase of 20 more of the double-decker jets based on a contract worth some £6.8 billion before discounts.

Refreshing the super jumbo

In an effort to revitalise flagging sales of the A380, Airbus has had to look at new ways of marketing the aircraft. Several airlines, Emirates in particular, have long wanted to see a 'neo' version (new engine option) but this looks to be some way off given an announcement made by Airbus at the Paris Air Show in June 2017.

It was here that Airbus announced the launch of a so-called 'development study' for what the manufacturer calls the 'A380plus'. The study sets out a series of aerodynamic improvements, in particular, large new winglets and other wing refinements that allow for up to 4% in fuel-burn savings. Winglets work by dissipating the vortices of rapidly spinning air created by the wings. They measure approximately 4.7m in height and comprise an uplet of 3.5m and a downlet of 1.2m. The new winglet is designed to improve aerodynamics and reduce drag.

Other upgrades for the A380plus announced by Airbus included:

- An increased MTOW of 578 tonnes providing the flexibility of carrying up to 80 more passengers over today's range (8,200nm), or flying 300nm further.
- Longer maintenance check intervals, a reduced six-year check downtime and systems improvements, which will lessen maintenance costs and increase aircraft availability.

Airbus projects the overall benefit of the new features is a 13% cost per seat reduction versus today's A380, which is good news for airlines.

John Leahy, Airbus COO Customers, said:

This is a new step for our iconic aircraft to best serve worldwide fast-growing traffic and the evolving needs of the A380 customers.

The A380 is well-proven as the solution to increasing congestion at large airports, and in offering a unique, passenger-preferred experience.

Prior to the Paris Air Show announcement, Airbus unveiled a possible change to the cabin design to raise the passenger count on the aircraft 'by around 80 seats with the same comfort level versus current deliveries'. Space occupied by the aircraft's large staircases – seen by many as inconsequential to the passenger experience – could be reclaimed or redesigned to enable new options for airlines to make further innovations across cabins of their choice. This idea is still being investigated to assess the potential complications it may bring to the boarding process as not all airports offer boarding to both decks.

The cabin layout proposals include a new 9-abreast seat configuration in premium economy and 11-abreast in economy, though this has received a mixed response from airlines. That said, the A380 does offer airlines an interesting option. For those carriers trying to maximise revenue by segmenting their planes into multiple classes, the A380's sheer size offers significant flexibility for a diverse cabin arrangement, particularly in the premium economy cabin which is proving a hit with passengers.

Separately, the idea of an A380 freighter version – initially launched with both Fedex and UPS – was shelved in 2007. Some industry commentators believe conversion to a freighter is a more complex task that initially envisioned, though Airbus remain tight-lipped about this.

New markets and alternative uses

Airbus remains positive about the potential for a second-hand market for the aircraft, with growing levels of interest among African, Chinese and some of the larger operators in the Middle East being open to taking older A380s. There is some scepticism about the potential of the second-hand market because residual values for the A380 are likely to be low, but even the likes of British Airways have expressed interest in buying second-hand models a decade after the A380 entered service in 2007.

ABOVE The A380plus was announced at the Paris Air Show in June 2017. *(Airbus)*

LEFT New winglets and other wing refinements enable improved fuel burn. *(Airbus)*

In an interesting development that has attracted a lot of headlines, Malaysia Airlines' six A380s will be transferred to a discrete operating company with a separate airline operator's licence. This is set to cater for the Hajj and Umrah pilgrimages to Mecca. In early 2018 the aircraft will be refitted with a flexible seating arrangement of 635 seats in a two-class configuration, or 720 for a one-class all-economy configuration. The move came after the carrier was unable to dispose of its A380s on the secondary market through sale or lease deals.

In mid-2017 news emerged that the A380

BELOW Benefits of the new A380plus upgrades. *(Airbus)*

A380 **plus** Even more efficient, still unique

Improved aerodynamics   Revenue space optimisation   Optimised maintenance

Up to **4**% fuel burn saving

Up to **80** more seats

13% cost per seat reduction

AIRBUS

may have found a new lease of life as an ultra-luxurious private jet when a European leasing company announced it would sell second-hand super jumbos as head-of-state aircraft.

The firm also announced that it would be commissioning a leading design agency to create the A380 private jet's opulent interior. The aircraft are believed to be the four early-build A380s coming off lease from Singapore Airlines. Some industry commentators believe the announcement could represent the beginning of a new phase for the A380.

Ahead of its time

The A380 has certainly had its critics, but considering it entered service at the same time as the financial crisis hit and soaring oil prices made airlines reluctant to buy big four-engine aircraft, many believe its success still lies ahead of it, given the growth in air travel and traffic predicted worldwide. Peter Bellew, Chief Executive of Malaysia Airlines remarked:

When you get into 2021, the growth and the congestion and the lack of runway development means the A380 will be a success, and it won't be down to the marketing of the aircraft, it will be the fact that global traffic will be off the chart and the plane will be required to use the airport slots that are available.

Other industry commentators share the same view that the A380's best years are in fact ahead of it and that it's far from being a plane whose time has come and gone.

With global airline traffic expected to continue growing at a rapid rate, at some point demand will undoubtedly catch up. That said, in the current climate, Airbus has little choice but to accept the slow commercial performance of the A380 but they firmly believe its time will come. 'There is a future with this aircraft: more airports will become like Heathrow with congestion and this aircraft will have a bigger market share – we simply have to shift to bigger aircraft and all economic indicators point to that,' said CEO Fabrice Brégier in a January 2017 interview.

Conclusion

The order book for the A380 may not currently reflect what Airbus had been hoping for, but ten years is too short a time to determine the fate of this remarkable aircraft. More than a decade after its maiden flight, it remains a major point of interest for airline industry insiders and passengers alike. Research shows some 60% of the 170 million passengers who have flown on the aircraft are ready to make an extra effort to do so again, giving it something of a cult following.

The aircraft certainly has its detractors and there are genuine concerns that if demand doesn't rebound within the next few years, the future of the A380 could be in real jeopardy.

BELOW An Etihad Airways A380 rolls out of the paint hangar during a launch ceremony in Hamburg (Finkenwerder) in September 2014. *(Airbus)*

BOTTOM The A380 is a marvel of modern aeronautical engineering and state-of-the-art technology. *(Lufthansa)*

Plans for a next-generation aircraft look to be at least a few years away and working towards profitability while maintaining market confidence by building one a month will be a significant challenge.

The focus for Airbus in the current market is to find new customers to support and maintain production levels for several more years. There is also scope for Airbus to refocus on the A380's utility, moving away from an aircraft with showers and bars to the initial concept – a high-density super jumbo designed to carry 600 or 700 people for ten hours between congested airports, making good use of congested slots at those airports and keeping the cost of travel down. This approach may be appealing to low-cost carriers, potentially making use of an all-economy-class A380.

Concerns aside, there is no getting away from the fact that this aircraft is a marvel of modern aeronautical engineering, state-of-the-art technology, innovation and comfort. By Airbus estimates, the size of the market demand for VLA looks set to reach 1,400 aircraft over the next 20 years, with more than half the demand coming from the Asia-Pacific region. The manufacturer cautiously predicts taking only half of the market and even if that number turns out to be smaller than Airbus is hoping for, the A380 looks likely to dominate, if not monopolise, long high-density routes for years to come.

LEFT The aircraft has developed a cult following, prompting Airbus to market the A380 to passengers in a couple of unique ways. *(Airbus)*

Doing so will enable the aircraft to produce a return on the investment made in the programme and for the A380 to take its rightful place in aviation history. That will be an outcome Airbus, its customer airlines and, in turn, their passengers will all be hoping for.

ABOVE More than a decade after its maiden flight, the A380 remains a major point of interest for airline industry insiders and passengers alike. *(Author)*

Demand for new passenger & freighter aircraft
Fleet in service evolution: 2017 - 2037
Passenger aircraft above 100 seats, freighter aircraft above 10 tonnes

The market demand for Very Large Aircraft (VLA) is forecast at around 1,500 aircraft over the next 20 years (of which Airbus targets some 50%)

LEFT Aircraft demand over the next twenty years looks set to continue apace. *(Author)*

Glossary

AC	Alternating Current	**DU**	Display Unit
ACMS	Aircraft Condition Monitoring System	**E/WD**	Engine/Warning Display
ADIRS	Air Data and Inertial Reference System	**EASA**	European Aviation Safety Agency
AFM	Aircraft Flight Manual	**EBCU**	Emergency Brake Control Unit
AFS	Auto Flight System	**EBHA**	Electrical Backup Hydraulic Actuator
AGS	Analysis Ground Station	**ECAM**	Electronic Centralised Aircraft Monitoring
A-ICE	Anti-Ice	**ECB**	Electronic Control Box
ALT	Altitude	**EFB**	Electronic Flight Bag
AOA	Angle-of-Attack	**EFF**	Electronic Flight Folder
AOG	Aircraft on Ground	**EFIS**	Electronic Flight Instrument System
AP	Autopilot	**EFOB**	Estimated Fuel on Board
APPR	Approach	**EHM**	Engine Health Management
APU	Auxiliary Power Unit	**EIS**	Entry into Service
ATC	Air Traffic Control	**E-Logbook**	
A/THR	Autothrust		Electronic Logbook
ATPL	Air Transport Pilot's Licence	**ELT**	Emergency Locator Transmitter
BAT	Battery	**ETA**	Estimated Time of Arrival
BCS	Brake Control System	**ETACS**	External Taxi Aid Camera System
BLG	Body Landing Gears	**ETOPS**	Extended Twin-Engine Operation Performance Standards
BWS	Body Wheel Steering		
C/B	Circuit Breaker	**EVAC**	Evacuation
C/L	Checklist	**EXT**	External
CAPT	Captain	**F/CTL**	Flight Controls
CCOM	Cabin Crew Operating Manual	**F/O**	First Officer
CDAM	Central Data Acquisition Module	**FAA**	Federal Aviation Authority (USA)
CDL	Configuration Deviation List	**FADEC**	Full Authority Digital Engine Control
CDS	Control and Display System	**FAP**	Flight Attendant Panel
CDSS	Cockpit Door Surveillance System	**FAR**	Federal Aviation Regulations
CFRP	Carbon Fibre Reinforced Plastic	**FCOM**	Flight Crew Operating Manual
CG	Centre of Gravity	**FCTM**	Flight Crew Training Manual
CL	Climb	**FCU**	Flight Control Unit
CLEDU	Cabin LED Units	**FDRS**	Flight Data Recording System
CMS	Central Maintenance System	**FDU**	Fire Detection Unit
CMV	Concentrator and Multiplexer for Video	**FE**	Flight Envelope
CP	Control Panel	**FL**	Flight Level
CPC	Cabin Pressure Controller	**FMC**	Flight Management Computer
CRZ	Cruise	**FMS**	Flight Management System
CVMS	Cabin Video Monitoring System	**FOM**	Flight Operations Manual
CVR	Cockpit Voice Recorder	**FQMS**	Fuel Quantity and Management System
DC	Direct Current		
DCLB	Derated Climb	**FWS**	Flight Warning System
DES	Descent	**G/S**	Glide slope
DLCS	Data Load and Configuration System		

GA	Go Around	**NAVAID**	(Radio) Navigation Aid
GEN	Generator	**ND**	Navigation Display
Glare™	Glass Laminate Aluminium Reinforced Epoxy	**NLG**	Nose Landing Gear
		NSS	Network Server System
GLS	GPS Landing System	**NWS**	Nosewheel Steering
GPS	Global Positioning System	**OANS**	Onboard Airport Navigation System
GPWS	Ground Proximity Warning System	**OIS**	Onboard Information System
GRAWDE		**OIT**	Onboard Information Terminal
	Gear Rib Automated Wing Drilling Equipment	**OMS**	Onboard Maintenance System
		OMT	Onboard Maintenance Terminal
HAWDE	Horizontal Automatic Wing Drilling Equipment	**PBE**	Protective Breathing Equipment
		PFD	Primary Flight Display
HCU	Head-up Combiner Unit	**PFR**	Post-Flight Report
HDG	Heading	**PMAT**	Portable Multipurpose Access Terminal
HP	High Pressure		
hp	Horsepower	**PTS**	Precision Time Schedule
HSMU	Hydraulic System Monitoring Unit	**RAT**	Ram Air Turbine
HUD	Head-Up Display	**RMP**	Radio Management Panel
HUDC	Head-Up Display Computer	**RWY**	Runway
HUPU	Head-Up Projection Unit	**SATCOM**	Satellite Communication
ICAO	International Civil Aviation Organisation	**SCI**	Secure Communication Interface
IFE	In-Flight Entertainment	**SCS**	Steering Control System
ILS	Instrument Landing System	**SD**	System Display
IMA	Integrated Modular Avionics	**SDF**	Smoke Detection Function
IP	Intermediate Pressure	**SID**	Standard Instrument Departure
ISIS	Integrated Standby Instrument System	**SOP**	Standard Operating Procedures
JAR	Joint Aviation Requirements	**SQWK**	Squawk
KCCU	Keyboard and Cursor Unit	**T/C**	Top of Climb
LA XFR	Load Alleviation Transfer	**T/D**	Top of Descent
LAF	Load Alleviation Function	**TAWS**	Terrain Awareness and Warning System
LCD	Liquid Crystal Display		
LCDU	Liquid Crystal Display Unit	**TCAS**	Traffic Collision Avoidance System
LGCIS	Landing Gear Control and Indicating System	**THR**	Thrust
		THS	Trimmable Horizontal Stabiliser
LGERS	Landing Gear Extension and Retraction System	**TK**	Tank
		TO	Take-off
LOC	Localiser	**UHCA**	Ultra High Capacity Airliner
LP	Low Pressure	**V/S**	Vertical Speed
LVER	Low Voltage Electro-magnetic Riveting	**VAPP**	Final Approach Speed
		VD	Vertical Display
MCT	Maximum Continuous Thrust	**VHF**	Very High Frequency
MEL	Minimum Equipment List	**VLCT**	Very Large Commercial Transport
MFD	Multi-Function Display	**VLR**	Very Long Range
MG	Maturity Gate	**VMO**	Maximum Operating Speed
MLG	Main Landing Gears	**W&B**	Weight and Balance
MLW	Maximum Landing Weight	**WLAN**	Wireless Local Area Network
MPV	Multi-Purpose Vehicle	**WLG**	Wing Landing Gears
MRO	Maintenance Repair and Overhaul	**WXR**	Weather Radar
MSN	Manufacturer Serial Number	**XFR**	Transfer
MTOW	Maximum Take-Off Weight	**ZFCG**	Zero Fuel Centre of Gravity
MZFW	Maximum Zero Fuel Weight	**ZFW**	Zero Fuel Weight
NAV	Navigation		

Index